TAGALOG
MADE EASY LEVEL 1

*An Easy Step-By-Step Approach
To Learn Tagalog for Beginners
(Textbook + Workbook Included)*

Lingo Mastery

ISBN: 978-1-951949-75-4

Copyright © 2023 by Lingo Mastery

ALL RIGHTS RESERVED

No part of this book may be reproduced, stored in a retrieval system, or transmitted in any form or by any means, electronic, mechanical, photocopying, recording, scanning, or otherwise, without the prior written permission of the publisher.
The illustrations in this book were designed using images from Freepik.com.

CONTENTS

Preface 1

Introduction 2

HOW TO GET THE AUDIO FILES 4

Section 1 – Get to know the Philippines 5

   A. GRAMMAR 6

      Exercise #1 13

      Listening #1 13

   B. VOCABULARY 14

      Exercise #2 18

      Exercise #3 22

      Exercise #4 24

      Listening #2 25

Section 2 – Greetings and questions 26

   A. GRAMMAR 27

      Exercise #1 29

      Exercise #2 37

      Listening #1 38

   B. VOCABULARY 39

      Exercise #3 44

      Exercise #4 50

      Listening #2 51

Section 3 – How well do you know yourself? 52

A. GRAMMAR 53

Exercise #1 55

Exercise #2 63

Listening #1 63

B. VOCABULARY 64

Exercise #3 67

Exercise #4 70

Exercise #5 73

Listening #2 75

Section 4 – Get to know others too 76

A. GRAMMAR 77

Exercise #1 80

Exercise #2 86

Exercise #3 92

Listening #1 93

B. VOCABULARY 94

Exercise #4 98

Listening #2 100

Section 5 – Come on, let's move around 101

A. GRAMMAR 102

Exercise #1 108

Exercise #2 115

Exercise #3 119

    Exercise #4 124

    Listening #1 125

    B. VOCABULARY 126

    Exercise #5 132

    Listening #2 135

Section 6 – Let's eat! 136

    Exercise #1 140

    Exercise #2 140

    Listening #1 142

Section 7 – What do you do? 143

    Exercise #1 146

    Exercise #2 147

    Listening #1 148

Section 8 – What can you say about...? 149

    Exercise #1 153

    Listening #1 154

Conclusion 155

Answer Key 156

PREFACE

With the long list of potential Asian languages to learn, Tagalog is a hidden gem that surprises most students with its linguistic richness. Statistics show that foreign learners are more interested in learning languages such as Korean, Japanese, and Chinese. While of course it is still a matter of preference, here are some reasons why Tagalog is often overlooked:

1. It does not have a 'unique' writing system like its neighboring languages such as Thai, Chinese, or Japanese.

2. With the **Philippines** having a whopping 180+ regional languages, most people think that Tagalog is not that widely used in the country anyway.

3. English is one of the country's official languages. Linguistic barriers are not so much of a problem, so most students feel like there's no use learning the native language.

While some of these things may hold true, one cannot deny the value of learning Tagalog. First, if you're visiting the Philippines, it is not guaranteed that your English will save the day. Remember, the Philippines is composed of many islands! Finding yourself on an island where people may not be well-versed in English can be your worst nightmare. Knowing the basics of Tagalog is your best bet when getting around.

Next, just because Tagalog does not have its own writing system does not mean it is less interesting. Digging deeper beyond orthography, you will be surprised at how rich the language is, with its unique expressions and other linguistic nuances that you will not find in the English language. From politeness markers to expressing emotions, the language will be your window to the Filipino heritage and culture.

So, who says Tagalog isn't interesting?

This vocabulary workbook was especially created to address the scarcity of innovative Tagalog resources. This is for the students who are tired of reading the old grammar books that only promote blind memorization instead of deep language acquisition. Every grammar and vocabulary lesson in this book will also reflect the life and culture of the Filipino people. This workbook will allow you to learn Tagalog not only as a language but as a nation's identity.

INTRODUCTION

This workbook employs a contextualized approach, where language is presented not only as a communication tool but as a cultural experience. You will learn about more than just the formal Tagalog grammar rules, phonetics, and vocabulary. You will be introduced to real-life situations where you can really grasp *how*, *where* and *when* certain words and expressions are used. This approach aims to develop your communication skills in natural, native conditions.

A BRIEF HISTORY OF TAGALOG

Tagalog belongs to the Austronesian language family, a language group which mainly developed on the islands and coasts of the Pacific Ocean. Most of the early studies of the Tagalog language trace back to the Spanish era in the Philippines. The first known Tagalog dictionaries were created and compiled by Spanish missionaries. When the 300-year Spanish rule ended, Tagalog was officially declared as the Philippines' national language.

Tagalog kept its status until the 1950s, when the name was changed to **Pilipino** in efforts to make the country's national language more inclusive. As there are more than 180 regional languages in the Philippines, many protested, wondering why Tagalog, mainly spoken in Central Luzon, was chosen as the national language. From Pilipino, it then shifted to **Filipino** in the 1973 Constitution. At present, Filipino, together with English, are mandated as the official languages of the Philippines.

As far as mutual intelligibility is concerned, there are no linguistic differences between Tagalog and Filipino. The separation of terms had more to do with its political implications, but the two languages share identical grammatical structures and lexical features. As some experts put it, the language is referred to as Tagalog within the Philippines to differentiate it among other Philippine languages, but the term Filipino is used more to differentiate it from other international languages.

WORKBOOK STRUCTURE

This workbook is a solid self-study device that will help learners effectively absorb the intricacies of the Tagalog language. The course is not just a list of English–Tagalog translations, but a simulation of real conversations that will further your knowledge about Tagalog and the Philippines in general.

Each chapter is divided into two components: grammar structures and vocabulary. The lessons are presented as themes, allowing students to immerse themselves in how the language is actually used by its native speakers. From being able to introduce yourself to traveling around, this book is a step-by-step guide that supports your linguistic progress in the most practical way. Each lesson then ends with a simple exercise that allows you to enhance your experience with the language.

The lessons on Tagalog phonetics, vocabulary, and common expressions are carefully curated to develop your communication skills at the initial level. They contain a perfect balance of pragmatic and challenging discussions. The complexity of the linguistic information included in this book has been controlled, so you don't have to worry about it being too hard for beginners.

TIPS AND RECOMMENDATIONS

Smart reading is the best way to approach self-studying a language. This means you create your own pace in absorbing the information presented in the book. You don't just memorize the words, you also put them into real contexts as you go over them.

Here are other tips to help you make the most out of your learning:

- Read at your own pace. The beauty of a self-study tool is that you don't have to rush to meet any deadlines. Language acquisition is not linear. You can go back and forth as much as you want. What's important is that you retain the knowledge in the long term.

- While Tagalog may have similarities with the structure of English, it is still best not to depend too much on your native language. There are numerous linguistic nuances in Tagalog that do not exist in English. The more you compare, the more you might get confused.

- After each chapter, try to add more to the list of vocabulary in this book. If the chapter's theme is traveling, do some research and add new words that you think are related to it. A personalized vocabulary will help you retain words better.

- Lastly, practice! It can't be stressed enough, but language learning is a repetitive process. There is no getting it the first time. You're supposed to make mistakes, you're supposed to miss a couple of steps—and that's okay. The journey won't be perfect, but you have to be consistent.

HOW TO GET THE AUDIO FILES

Some of the exercises throughout this book come with accompanying audio files. You can download these audio files if you head over to
www.lingomastery.com/tagalog-me1-audio

KILALANIN MO ANG PILIPINAS
GET TO KNOW THE PHILIPPINES

The first section of this book takes you to the basics of Tagalog. You will be introduced to the phonetics and orthography of the language. This section will also include the types of loanwords you will find in Tagalog. For the vocabulary part, you will get to know more about the Philippines by learning about its places, weather, and people. You will also learn how to express numbers, dates, and days.

A. GRAMMAR

TAGALOG VOWELS AND CONSONANTS

The official Tagalog alphabet is comprised of 28 letters–26 of which are shared with English. The additional two are ñ /enye/ and ng /nga/. Although there are a lot of orthographic similarities with English, Tagalog sounds may still vary greatly from it.

VOWELS (PATINIG)

LETTER	IPA	AS IN...	TAGALOG EXAMPLES
Aa	/a/	arm, palm, abort	aso (dog), nanay (mother), bata (child)
Ee	/ɛ/	bed, step, end	keso (cheese), pero (but), relo (watch)
Ii	/i/	pin, simple, eel	ilaw (light), pinto (door), isda (fish)
Oo	/ɔ/	onset, osteoporosis, poll	oso (bear), pondo (fund), takbo (run)
Uu	/u/	pool, bull, put	usok (smoke), buto (bone), mundo (world)

Just like in English, vowel lengths in Tagalog are very important. For example, the vowel length between *steel* and *still* makes all the difference in their meaning. This is also the case with Tagalog, tubo /TOO-bo/ means pipe while tubo /tu-BO/ means sugarcane.

Another thing to be careful about is pronouncing the Tagalog **o** and **u**. Notice how in the word *osteoporosis* /os-te-yo-po-ROW-sis/, the last o was not underlined. This is because Tagalog **o** is not phonetically the same as **o** /ow/ in words such as *go* /gow/ or *stone* /stown/. As for the vowel **u**, it cannot be pronounced as /yu/ as in *universal* or /uh/ as in *cut*.

CONSONANTS (KATINIG)

LETTER	IPA	AS IN...	TAGALOG EXAMPLES
Bb	/b/	baby, belt	**baka** (*cow*), **pabuya** (*prize*)
Cc *loanwords	/si/, /k/, /tʃ/	come, avocado	**abaca** (*a type of Philippine plant*)
Dd	/d/	doll, drink	**damdamin** (*feeling*), **dilaw** (*yellow*)
Ff *loanwords	/f/	fish, flu	**Ifugao** (*landlocked province of the Philippines in the Cordillera Administrative Region in Luzon*)
Gg	/g/	gamble, grow	**gusali** (*building*), **gusto** (*like*)
Hh	/h/	house, help	**hilaw** (*raw*), **hugas** (*wash*)
Jj *loanwords	/dʒ/, /h/	jump, Jose	**hija/hijo** (*young girl or boy*)
Kk	/k/	kill, back	**kumot** (*blanket*), **karne** (*meat*)
Ll	/l/	lemon, love	**lima** (*five*), **laban** (*fight*)
Mm	/m/	make, miss	**minsan** (*sometimes*), **mura** (*cheap*)
Nn	/n/	name, not	**narito** (*here*), **pinsan** (*cousin*)
Ññ *loanwords	/nj/	señorita	**Santo Niño** (*religious icon of baby Jesus*)
Ng	/ŋ/	ring, lung	**ngayon** (*now*), **panga** (*jaw*)
Pp	/p/	post, pet	**prito** (*fry*), **pusa** (*cat*)
Qq *loanwords	/k/	Quebec	**Quezon** (*last name of the second President of the Philippines*)
Rr	/r/	rich, rain	**relo** (*watch*), **pares** (*pair*)
Ss	/s/	sick, supreme	**samba** (*worship*), **sugal** (*gamble*)
Tt	/t/	top, tell	**tainga** (*ear*), **tingin** (*look*)
Vv *loanwords	/v/	very, valve	**Ivatan** (*an ethnolinguistic group native to Batanes and Babuyan Islands of the northernmost Philippines*)
Ww	/w/	welcome, wait	**wala** (*none*), **walis** (*broom*)
Xx *loanwords	/s/, /ks/	xylophone	xerox
Yy	/j/	yank, yacht	**yelo** (*ice*), **tatay** (*father*)
Zz *loanwords	/tʒ/	zebra	pizza

As you may notice, there are consonants in Tagalog that are only used for loanwords. Letters **c, f, j, ñ, q, v, x,** and **z** were officially added through the 1987 Constitution to push for a "Modern Filipino Alphabet". These phonemes are non-native and are of Spanish origin.

A general note for pronouncing Tagalog consonants is to remove aspiration. Aspiration is the brief release of air that English speakers often make after consonants such as **t**, **k** and **p**. Examples for this are *cat* /kʰet/, *pan* /pʰen/, and *tall* /tʰal/.

The Tagalog **r** is different from the English **r** too. Tagalog **r** is made by rolling the tip of your tongue against the roof of your mouth, or what we call the trill **r**. On the other hand, English **r** is called a retroflex **r** where your tongue is curled far back in your mouth. If you are still confused, try to say the word *mother* and observe what position your tongue ends up in. It's curled, right? That's a retroflex **r** right there. You can practice the Tagalog **r** by putting the tip of your tongue near your upper teeth and making the *grrrr* sound. You gotta roll those r's!

Next is the **ng** sound. *Sing, lung, long*–you might think that this is such an easy sound to make. Wait until it gets to the beginning or middle of the word. Most English speakers find it hard to pronounce the **ng** sound when it's not in a syllable-final position. Words like **ngipin** /NGEE-pin/ '*tooth*' and **pangalan** /pa-NGA-lan/ '*name*' are actually quite challenging for Tagalog learners. To practice, take the word sing-along and repeat it fast. When you pronounce *singalong* as if it's one word, you'll get the hang of the **ng** sound in Tagalog.

DIPHTHONGS

Diphthongs are complex sounds that are a combination of two vowel sounds or semi-vowel sounds, as in c<u>oi</u>n *[oy]* and <u>ai</u>r *[ey]*. There are five diphthongs in Tagalog:

LETTER	IPA	AS IN...	TAGALOG EXAMPLES
aw	/aw/	loud	**araw** (*day/sun*)
ay	/aj/	light	**patay** (*dead*)
iw	/iw/	N/A (sounds like the slang *eww*)	**aliw** (*fun*)
oy	/ɔj/	soil	**baboy** (*pig*)
uy	/uj/	N/A (sounds like the Spanish word *muy*)	**baduy** (*unfashionable*)

DIGRAPHS

Digraphs are two letters that form a single sound. An example is **ph**, which sounds like an **f**. Tagalog digraphs are **sy**, **dy**, **ts**, **ty**, and **ny**.

LETTER	IPA	AS IN...	TAGALOG EXAMPLES
sy	/ʃ/	shout, shell	**siya/sya** (he/she), **pasya** (decision)
dy	/dʒ/	joke, jump	**diyan/dyan** (there), **dyaryo** (newspaper)
ts, ty	/tʃ/	change, charm	**tsinelas** (slippers), **tsokolate** (chocolate), **tiyan/tyan** (stomach)
ny	/nj/	señor	**pinya** (pineapple), **panyo** (handkerchief)

Some of these digraphs reflect localized pronunciation of loanwords such as *pizza* [pitsa], *chocolate* [tsokolate] and *jeep* [dyip].

GLOTTAL STOP

The glottal stop is an integral part of Tagalog phonetics. Its presence or absence can change the entire meaning of a word.

To put it simply, glottal stop is the sudden restriction of air in your throat before or after pronouncing a vowel. It is represented by the symbol /ʔ/ in the International Phonetic Alphabet or IPA. The glottal stop can be a complex concept for English speakers, so let's try to break it down. To understand it better, think of the slang words *na-ah* or *uh-oh*. Notice how you stop in the middle? That's the glottal stop right there.

It is important to know which words in Tagalog end with glottal stop. As mentioned, a mistake in pronouncing the glottal stop can shift the meaning of your message. For example:

WORD	PRONUNCIATION	MEANING
basa (no glottal stop)	/BA-sa/	to read
basa (with glottal stop)	/ba-SAʔ/	wet
tubo (no glottal stop)	/TOO-bo/	pipe
tubo (with glottal stop)	/TOO-boʔ/	profit

To practice the glottal stop, try to immediately cut yourself off and hold your breath when you are pronouncing the syllable where the stop is placed. This is especially useful when you encounter double vowels such as **maanghang** /ma-ang-HANG/ *'spicy'* or **leeg** /le-EG/ *'neck'* where glottal stops separate the two vowels.

SYLLABLE STRESS

In relation to the glottal stop, the position of your syllable stress also determines the meaning of Tagalog words. Examples are:

WORD	PRONUNCIATION	MEANING
baon	/BA-on/	allowance
baon	/ba-ON/	to bury
upo	/oo-PO/	to sit
upo	/OO-po/	bottle gourd
buhay	/BOO-hay/	life
buhay	/boo-HAY/	alive
aso	/A-so/	dog
aso	/a-SO/	smoke

Tagalog phonetics and orthography may be a bit overwhelming at first, but as you practice, you will realize that these words are actually pretty easy to get used to. Tagalog is not a tonal language, unlike other Asian languages. You just need to familiarize yourself with its individual vowel and consonant sounds. After that, you'll see that most words are read as they are spelled. As for the variation in meanings, you will learn more about it as you dive deeper into Tagalog and its social contexts.

TAGALOG LOANWORDS

Now, let's talk about how Tagalog loanwords are derived and pronounced. Because of their historical ties with the Philippines, Spanish and English have the biggest influences on Tagalog. While most of these loanwords have undergone orthographic and phonetic changes, they are still considered near cognates.

SPANISH ORIGIN

SPANISH	TAGALOG	MEANING
alcalde	alkalde	*mayor*
baño	banyo	*bathroom*
cocina	kusina	*kitchen*
diario	diyaryo	*newspaper*
hebra	hibla	*strand*
cebollas	sibuyas	*onion*
silla	silya	*chair*
caballo	kabayo	*horse*
barba	balbas	*beard*
cómo estás	kumusta	*how are you*
apellido	apelyido	*surname*
ventana	bintana	*window*
cinturón	sinturon	*belt*
lavabo	lababo	*sink*
brazo	braso	*arm*

There are also loanwords that underwent a semantic shift over time. This means that these words did not retain their original meaning from the source language. Some loanwords may still be related to the original word to some extent.

SPANISH	MEANING	TAGALOG	MEANING
barcada	*boat trip*	**barkada**	*circle of friends*
almorzar	*to have lunch*	**almusal**	*breakfast*
código	*code*	**kodigo**	*cheat sheet*
cubeta	*bucket*	**kubeta**	*toilet*
siempre	*always*	**siyempre**	*of course*
corriente	*current*	**kuryente**	*electricity*
corazonada	*hunch, gut*	**kursonada**	*object of interest*
desgracia	*misfortune*	**disgrasya**	*accident*
seguro	*sure, certain*	**siguro**	*maybe*

Now let's move on to English-derived loanwords.

ENGLISH	TAGALOG
addict	adik
nurse	nars
interview	interbyu
chemical	kemikal
administration	administrasyon
curtain	kurtina
wise	wais
bicycle	bisikleta
stand by	tambay
plastic	plastik
police	pulis

EXERCISE #1

Isulat ang katumbas ng mga hiram na salita sa Ingles.
Write the English equivalent of the loanwords below.

1. alkalde _____
2. almusal _____
3. administrasyon _____
4. bisikleta _____
5. banyo _____
6. diyaryo _____
7. disgrasya _____
8. interbyu _____
9. kusina _____
10. kuryente _____

11. kemikal _____
12. kurtina _____
13. lababo _____
14. barkada _____
15. nars _____
16. plastik _____
17. pulis _____
18. kodigo _____
19. tambay _____
20. wais _____

 LISTENING #1 (Find audio on page 4.)

Makinig nang mabuti at isulat ang mga salitang binabanggit.
Listen carefully and write the words dictated in the audio.

1. _____
2. _____
3. _____
4. _____
5. _____

6. _____
7. _____
8. _____
9. _____
10. _____

B. VOCABULARY

Learning Tagalog and getting to know the Philippines calls for familiarizing ourselves with its geography, weather, and people. In this section, you will learn how to get around the country by being able to express common places or cities, directions, weather, and numbers.

PLACES AND DIRECTIONS

The Philippines is an archipelago in Southeast Asia. It is comprised of three major islands: **Luzon, Visayas, and Mindanao**. Its capital is Manila City, or in Tagalog, **Lungsod ng Maynila**.

First things first: public transportation. If you want to travel around the Philippines, it is extremely important that you know basic commuting terms and expressions. The most common means of transportation in the Philippines are:

Bus – **Bus** *(pronounced as boos)*

There are two types of buses in the Philippines: city and provincial buses. City buses are those that operate in Metro Manila, and provincial buses are those that operate outside of the main city.

Train – **Tren**

Filipinos refer to their major train systems as **MRT** *(Mass Rapid Transit),* **LRT** *(Light-Rail Transit), and* **PNR** *(Philippine National Railways) Metro Commuter Line. These trains only operate in Metro Manila. In 2009, PNR Bicol Commuter was launched to serve passengers in the provinces of Naga and Legazpi and limited to one train a day.*

Tricycle – **Traysikel**

This three-wheeled motorcycle is commonly found on smaller roads and is not allowed on highways.

Jeep – **Dyip**

The jeepney, commonly referred to as "jeep" is the most typical form of public transportation. It can fit 20 to 25 passengers. If you want to get off, you must say **"Para!"** *to signal the driver to stop.*

Sidecar/Pedicab – **Pedikab/Padyak** *(pronounced as pa-JAK)*

The sidecar usually operates in narrow streets or small communities/villages.

There are two ways that you can ask for directions:

1. **Saan po ang (pangalan ng lugar)?** = *Where is (name of the place)?*
2. **Paano po pumunta sa (pangalan ng lugar)?** = *How do I get to (name of the place)?*

Examples:

1. **Saan po ang sakayan ng bus?** = *Where is the bus stop?*
2. **Paano po pumunta sa Maynila?** = *How do I get to Manila?*

COMMON PLACES

bahay – *house*
simbahan – *church*
ospital – *hospital*
paaralan/eskwelahan – *school*
opisina – *office*
parke – *park*

POPULAR DESTINATIONS IN THE PHILIPPINES

Manila
Makati
Bonifacio Global City

Cebu
Davao
Boracay

Intramuros
Palawan
Tagaytay

Baguio
Siargao
Bohol

DIRECTIONS/POSITIONS

kanan – *right*
kaliwa – *left*
taas – *up/on top*
baba – *down/below*
hilaga – *north*
timog – *south*
silangan – *east*
kanluran – *west*
malapit – *near*
malayo – *far*
katabi – *beside/next to*

sa harap – *in front*
sa likod – *at the back*
katapat – *across*
sa loob – *inside*
sa labas – *outside*
sa susunod na kanto – *on the next street corner*
sa kabilang kanto – *on the other street corner*
sa gilid – *on the side*
diretso – *straight ahead*
gitna – *center*

If you want to say that you are in a certain place, use the word **nasa**:
Nasa Boracay ako. = *I am in Boracay.*
Nasa bahay si John. = *John is in the house.*
Nasa labas ang pusa. = *The cat is outside.*
Nasa kanan ng gusali ang kotse. = *The car is on the right side of the building.*

EXERCISE #2

Base sa mga larawan, tukuyin ang direksyon o posisyon ng bilog sa Tagalog.
Based on the illustrations, describe the position of the dot in Tagalog.

1.

2.

3.

4.

5.

NUMBERS, DATES, TIME

Another thing that will help you get around is knowing your numerical expressions. This includes the terms for days, dates, and time.

COUNTING NUMBERS

isa – *one*
dalawa – *two*
tatlo – *three*
apat – *four*
lima – *five*

anim – *six*
pito – *seven*
walo – *eight*
siyam – *nine*
sampu – *ten*

To form 11, 12, 13, etc., you just add the word **labing** to the number, as in:

labing-isa – *eleven*
labindalawa – *twelve*
labintatlo – *thirteen*
labing-apat – *fourteen*
labinlima – *fifteen*
labing-anim – *sixteen*
labimpito – *seventeen*
labing-walo – *eighteen*
labing-siyam – *nineteen*

Please note that **labing** undergoes phonetic assimilation in certain numbers as seen in **labing** + **dalawa** = **labindalawa** and **labing** + **pito** = **labimpito**.

20s, 30s, 40s, etc. are formed by adding **-napu** or **-mpu** at the end of the number. **-Napu** is added to numbers ending in consonants, while **-mpu** is added to numbers ending in vowels.

dalawampu – *twenty*
tatlumpu – *thirty*
apatnapu – *forty*
limampu – *fifty*

animnapu – *sixty*
pitumpu – *seventy*
walumpu – *eighty*
siyamnapu – *ninety*

Hundreds, thousands, millions, etc. are formed by adding **-ng/na** plus **daan**, **libo**, **milyon** to the number. **"-Ng"** is used for numbers ending in vowels, while **"na"** is used for numbers ending in consonants.

isang daan – *one hundred*
dalawang daan – *two hundred*
tatlong libo – *three thousand*

apat na libo – *four thousand*
limang milyon – *five million*
anim na milyon – *six million*

ORDINAL NUMBERS

To express order, just add **ika-** or **pang-** to the number, except the number one.

una – *first*
ikalawa/pangalawa – *second*
ikatlo/pangatlo – *third*
ikaapat/pang-apat – *fourth*
ikalima/panlima – *fifth*

ikaanim/pang-anim – *sixth*
ikapito/pampito – *seventh*
ikawalo/pangwalo – *eighth*
ikasiyam/pangsiyam – *ninth*
ikasampu/pangsampu – *tenth*

Just like the other affixes, phonetic assimilation also occurs here, as in the cases of **pan** + **lima** = *panlima* and **pang** + **pito** = **pampito**.

Now let's move on to expressing the days and months in Tagalog.

DAYS

Lunes – *Monday*
Martes – *Tuesday*
Miyerkules – *Wednesday*
Huwebes – *Thursday*
Biyernes – *Friday*
Sabado – *Saturday*
Linggo - *Sunday*

MONTHS

Enero – *January*
Pebrero – *February*
Marso – *March*
Abril – *April*
Mayo – *May*
Hunyo – *June*
Hulyo – *July*
Agosto – *August*
Setyembre – *September*
Oktubre – *October*
Nobyembre – *November*
Disyembre - *December*

So, how do you express dates in Tagalog? The formula is <u>ordinal number + **ng** + month</u>. See the examples below:

ika-labingwalo ng Mayo = *18th of May*
ikatlo ng Disyembre = *3rd of December*
ika-siyam ng Hunyo = *9th of June*

This is the same formula used in expressing time in Tagalog.

ika-labing-isa ng <u>umaga</u> = *11 <u>AM</u> (morning)*
ikatlo ng <u>hapon</u> = *3 <u>PM</u> (afternoon)*
ikapito ng <u>gabi</u> = *7 <u>PM</u> (evening)*

It is important to note, however, that expressing dates and time in full Tagalog may sound too formal for native speakers. Since English is also considered an everyday language in the Philippines, numerical expressions, especially date and time, are best stated in English to sound more natural in a conversation. Moreover, Spanish equivalents are also frequently used to express date and time in the Philippines.

Examples:

ala-una **ng umaga** = *1 AM*
alas-dos **ng hapon** = *2 PM*
alas-onse **ng gabi** = *11 PM*

a-tres **ng Pebrero** = *February 3*
a-kinse **ng Nobyembre** = *November 15*
a-trenta'y uno **ng Enero** = *January 31*

EXERCISE #3

A. Ilista ang mga buwan ayon sa pagkakasunud-sunod.
List the names of the months according to their order.

1. _____
2. _____
3. _____
4. _____
5. _____
6. _____
7. _____
8. _____
9. _____
10. _____
11. _____
12. _____

Nobyembre	Pebrero	Agosto
Enero	Hulyo	Disyembre
Mayo	Marso	Hunyo
Setyembre	Abril	Oktubre

B. Pagtugmain ang mga sumusunod na bilang.
Match the following numbers.

7 •   • isa
3 •   • walo
9 •   • lima
1 •   • siyam
4 •   • pito
8 •   • sampu
2 •   • apat
10 •   • tatlo
5 •   • anim
6 •   • dalawa

WEATHER

Just like in any other culture, the topic of weather is always a foolproof choice in initiating small talk. There are only two seasons in the Philippines: the hot season and the rainy season. They are called **tag-init** and **tag-ulan**, respectively.

Here are some useful expressions that you can use to talk about the weather:

Kumusta ang panahon ngayong araw? = *How's the weather today?*
Maaraw ba sa labas? = *Is it sunny outside?*
Mukhang uulan mamaya. = *It looks like it's going to rain later.*
Sobrang init ngayon. = *It's so hot right now.*
Magdala ka ng payong. = *Bring an umbrella.*
Makulimlim ang langit. = *The sky is gloomy.*
Mahamog dito. = *It's foggy here.*
Maaliwalas ang panahon. = *The weather is great/clear.*

WEATHER VOCABULARY:

araw – *sun*
maaraw – *sunny*
ulap – *cloud*
maulap – *cloudy*
langit – *sky*
mainit – *hot*
malamig – *cold*
ulan – *rain*

maulan – *rainy*
ambon – *drizzle*
bagyo – *storm*
baha – *flood*
hamog – *fog*
makulimlim – *gloomy*
hangin – *wind*
mahangin – *windy*

Since the Philippines is a tropical country, expect year-round heat, especially during the months of April and May!

EXERCISE #4

Piliin ang salitang pinaka-angkop sa panahon na nasa larawan.
Choose the word that is most appropriate for the weather in the picture.

1.

a. maulan   b. maaraw   c. baha

4.

a. mainit   b. ulan   c. maulap

2.

a. baha   b. bagyo   c. makulimlim

5.

a. baha   b. hamog   c. mahangin

3.

a. mahangin   b. ambon   c. malamig

LISTENING #2 (Find audio on page 4.)

Pakinggan ang usapan ng magkaibang Dennis at Cathy at bilugan ang titik ng tamang sagot sa mga katanungan.

Listen to the conversation between Dennis and Cathy and answer the questions by encircling the letter of the correct answer.

1. What time of the day did Dennis call Cathy?

    a. morning b. afternoon c. evening

2. What time is Dennis' birthday celebration?

    a. 4 PM b. 5 PM c. 6 PM

3. Where is Taal Vista located?

    a. Manila b. Tagaytay c. Pasay

4. When is Dennis' birthday?

    a. June 11 b. June 12 c. June 13

5. What day of the week is Dennis' birthday?

    a. Sunday b. Monday c. Tuesday

Now that you've gotten to know more about the Philippines, it's time to move to some self-introduction. The grammar section covers politeness markers, basic greetings, and pronouns. For the vocabulary section, you'll learn to describe yourself by stating your nationality, work, age, family and hobbies. Lastly, you will also learn how to ask questions and express your moods/emotions.

A. GRAMMAR

POLITENESS MARKERS

Before anything else, it is very important that you learn how to express politeness in Tagalog. Filipinos are very particular about the virtue of respect, especially to elders. This is even reflected in their language. There are two politeness words in Tagalog: **opo** and **po**.

Opo is the polite version of **oo**, which means yes. So, if you're saying yes to someone who is older than you, you should use **opo** instead of **oo**. On the other hand, **po** is added to sentences to make it sound more polite. For example, if you want to say no politely, you ought to say **hindi po** instead of just **hindi** which means no.

The positioning of **po** within a sentence varies but is mostly placed after the subject or the head of the sentence, and at the end of the sentence.

Examples:

Si Maria po ang kumain ng mangga.
It is Maria who ate the mango. (Polite)

Nagpunta po ako sa sinehan.
I went to the cinema. (Polite)

Opo, ako po ang nagbigay ng pagkain sa pusa.
Yes, I was the one who gave food to the cat. (Polite)

Magandang umaga po!
Good morning! (Polite)

Tao po!
An expression that is equivalent to *"Is anybody there/home?" (Polite)*

BASIC GREETINGS

Ready to start a conversation? Let's start with the greetings! Remember, you can add *po* at the end of each greeting to make it polite!

Kumusta?	*How are you?*
Magandang umaga	*Good morning*
Magandang tanghali	*Good afternoon (usually used at noon)*
Magandang hapon	*Good afternoon (usually used later in the afternoon, as in 2 PM onwards)*
Magandang gabi	*Good evening*
Magandang araw	*Good day*

Other common expressions are:

Salamat	*Thank you*
Walang anuman	*Welcome*
Maligayang Pagdating	*Welcome (to a place)*
Maligayang Pagbabalik	*Welcome back*
Pakiusap	*Please*
Pasensya na	*Sorry*
Pagbati	*Congratulations*
Paalam	*Goodbye*
Ingat	*Take care*

And if you're looking for occasion-specific greetings, here are some examples:

Maligayang kaarawan	*Happy Birthday*
Maligayang Pasko	*Merry Christmas*
Maligayang Bagong Taon	*Happy New Year*
Manigong Bagong Taon	*Have a Prosperous New Year*
Pakikiramay	*Condolences*
Maligayang Kapistahan	*Happy Fiesta/Feast*
Maligayang Araw ng mga Puso	*Happy Valentine's Day*
Maligayang Anibersaryo	*Happy Anniversary*

EXERCISE #1

Piliin ang tamang pagbati sa pamamagitan ng pagsulat ng titik sa patlang.
Choose the correct greeting by writing the letter in the blank.

A. "Maligayang Pasko!"
B. "Magandang umaga."
C. "Maligayang Araw ng mga Puso."
D. "Maligayang Kaarawan."
E. "Maligayang Bagong Taon." / "Manigong Bagong Taon."
F. "Magandang gabi."
G. "Maligayang Anibersaryo."
H. "Maligayang pagbabalik."
I. "Maligayang Kapistahan."
J. "Magandang hapon."

_____ 1. You just woke up and saw your mom.

_____ 2. You are visiting your friend's family on the 25th of December.

_____ 3. It's the Feast of the Patron Saint in your town.

_____ 4. You entered a meeting in the afternoon.

_____ 5. You are meeting up with your Valentine date.

_____ 6. It's your sister's birthday.

_____ 7. A relative just came back from a vacation.

_____ 8. Your parents are celebrating 40 years of marriage.

_____ 9. You are meeting up with someone at dinnertime.

_____ 10. You are celebrating January 1st with your family.

PRONOUNS

Another vital part of your self-introduction is personal pronouns. While there are no gender-based pronouns in Tagalog, you still have to pay close attention to their grammatical cases, plurality, and POV (point of view). Unlike in English where it's just she/her or he/his, Tagalog can have multiple variations for a single word. We understand that Tagalog pronouns may be tricky to learn, so feel free to read this section at your own pace. You don't need to absorb every bit of information all at once!

Here's a table of Tagalog pronouns that you need to remember:

SINGULAR	PLURAL
FIRST PERSON	
Ako – I/Me **Ko** – My/Me **Akin** – Mine **Kita** – Me to You (Special)	*(speaker and you)* **Tayo** – We/Us **Natin** – Our **Atin** – Ours *(speaker and other people not including you)* **Kami** – We/Us **Namin** – We/Our **Amin** – Ours
SECOND PERSON	
Ikaw – You **Ka** – You **Mo** – You/Your **Iyo** – Yours	**Kayo** – You **Ninyo** – Your **Inyo** – You/Your/Yours
THIRD PERSON	
Siya – He/She, Him/Her **Niya** – His/Her **Kaniya** – His/Hers	**Sila** – They/Them **Nila** – Their **Kanila** – Their/Theirs

FIRST PERSON PRONOUNS (SINGULAR)

First person pronouns are those that refer to the speaker and the speaker's company such as *I, me, us, we, etc.*

First is **ako**. **Ako** could mean both *I* (doer of the action/subject) or *me* (beneficiary of the action).

Examples:
Ako ay maganda. = *I am beautiful. (Subject)*
Kumain ako ng mansanas. = *I ate an apple. (Subject, doer of the action)*

Mahal mo ba ako? = *Do you love me?(Beneficiary of the action)*
Binigyan ako ng bulaklak ni Peter. = *Peter gave me flowers. (Beneficiary of the action)*

Ko is generally used to indicate possession, as in *my*. This possessive pronoun comes after the noun. However, it could also function as two more things: a shortened form of **ako ('ko)** in certain cases, or the doer of the action in the passive voice, as in *me*.

Examples:
Kinuha niya ang panyo ko. = *He/She took my handkerchief. (Possessive)*
Ang aso ko ay mataba. = *My dog is fat. (Possessive)*

Nagpunta (a)'ko sa bahay ni Amy. = *I went to Amy's house. (Shortened form of ako)*
Tinawagan niya (a)'ko. = *He/She called me. (Shortened form of ako)*

Ang pitaka ay ibinalik ko. = *The wallet was returned by me. (Doer of the action in passive voice)*
Isinuko ko ang bandila. = *The flag was surrendered by me. (Doer of the action in passive voice)*

The last singular pronoun for the first person POV is **akin**. It has the same grammatical function as **ko** in the sense that it is used to indicate possession (mine). This pronoun could also function as *me*, the beneficiary of the action, when paired with the word **sa** (to).

Examples:
Akin ang teleponong iyan. = *That telephone is mine. (Possessive)*
Ang lahat ng nakikita mo ay akin. = *Everything that you see is mine. (Possessive)*

Ibigay mo sa akin ang sulat. = *Give me the letter. (Beneficiary of the action)*
Pinadala ni Jose ang pera sa akin. = *Jose sent me the money. (Beneficiary of the action)*

FIRST PERSON PRONOUNS (PLURAL)

There are two types of plural pronouns in the first person point of view: inclusive and exclusive. The first one includes the person the speaker is talking to (*us = you and I*), and exclusive does not include the person the speaker is talking to (*us = me and my friends without you*). Let's discuss inclusive first.

Tayo is used as a subject pronoun and the doer of the action.

Examples:
Tayo ay matalino. = *We (you and I) are smart. (Subject)*
Pupunta tayo sa Amerika. = *We (you and I) are going to America. (Subject, Doer of the action)*

The pronouns **natin** and **atin** are generally used to indicate possession (our and ours). However, **natin** can also function as the doer of the action in passive sentences.

Examples:
Ang pamilya natin ay masaya. = *Our (your and my) family is happy. (Possessive)*
Nilinis ko ang bahay natin. = *I cleaned our (your and my) house. (Possessive)*

Ang kotseng ito ay atin. = *This car is ours (yours and mine). (Possessive)*
Atin ang gusaling ito. = *This building is ours (yours and mine). (Possessive).*

Ang babae ay tinulungan natin. = *The woman was helped by us (you and me). (Doer of the action in passive voice)*

Ang tula ay isinulat natin. = *The poem was written by us (you and me). (Doer of the action in passive voice).*

Now let's move on to the exclusive type of *we/us*. Again, these pronouns refer to the speaker and another group of people that does not include the person they are speaking to.

Kami is typically used as a subject and doer of the action. However, it can also function as the beneficiary of the action.

Examples:
Kami ay mga doktor. = *We (me and my friends) are doctors. (Subject)*
Kami ay mag-aaral mamaya. = *We (me and my friends) are going to study later. (Subject, doer of the action)*

Binigyan nila kami ng pabuya. = *They gave us (me and my friends) a reward. (Beneficiary of the action)*
Nginitian kami ng bata. = *The baby smiled at us (me and my friends). (Beneficiary of the action)*

The exclusive pronouns **namin** and **amin** are used to express possession (our and ours). **Namin** can also function as the doer of the action in passive voice.

Examples:
Nawawala ang gamit namin. = *Our (me and my friends') things are missing. (Possessive)*
Ang anibersaryo namin ay sa ikalima ng Abril. = *Our (me and my partner's) anniversary is on April 5. (Possessive)*

Amin ang lupang iyon. = *That lot/land is ours (me and my family's). (Possessive)*
Ang amin ay amin. = *What's ours is ours. (Possessive)*

Ang bata ay sinagip namin. = *The child was rescued by us. (Doer of the action in passive voice)*
Ang utang na ito ay binayaran namin. = *This debt was paid by us. (Doer of the action in passive voice)*

FIRST PERSON PRONOUN (REFLEXIVE)

There is a special pronoun in Tagalog that expresses an action done by me to you. This is called **kita**. This pronoun usually comes after the verb.

Examples:
Mahal kita. = *I love you.*
Sunduin kita bukas? = *Shall I pick you up tomorrow?*
Tinawagan kita kanina. = *I called you a while ago.*
Hihintayin kita. = *I will wait for you.*

SECOND PERSON PRONOUNS (SINGULAR)

Second person pronouns are those that refer to the person or group of people that the speaker is talking to. Examples are *you, your, yours, etc.*

In Tagalog, the singular you is **ikaw**. It is generally used as a subject pronoun and doer of the action.

Examples:
Ikaw ay maganda. = *You are beautiful. (Subject)*
Ikaw ang kumuha ng aking sapatos. = *You took my shoes. (Subject, doer of the action)*

Mo and **iyo**, on the other hand, are equivalent to the possessive *your* and *yours*. **Mo** could also mean *you* as the doer of the action but can never be a subject of a Tagalog sentence. **Iyo** can also act as a beneficiary of an action.

Examples:
Responsibilidad mo ang buhay mo. = *Your life is your responsibility. (Possessive)*
Alam ko na ang sikreto mo. = *I already know your secret. (Possessive)*
Sa iyo ang relong ito. = *This watch is yours. (Possessive)*
Ang gantimpalang ito ay iyo. = *This reward is yours. (Possessive)*

Binigay mo ba ang sobre sa kaniya? = *Did you give the envelope to him? (Doer of the action)*
Sabihin mo kung ano ang gusto mo. = *(You) tell me what you want. (Doer of the action)*
Binigay ba sa iyo ang sobre? = *Was the envelope given to you? (Beneficiary of the action)*
Ang kantang ito ay alay ko sa iyo. = *I offer this song to you. (Beneficiary of the action)*

Another second person pronoun is **ka**. It is used as an object pronoun or the receiver of the action. Just like **mo**, it can never be a subject in Tagalog sentences.

Examples:
Mahal ka ni Steve. = *Steve loves you. (Receiver of the action)*
Binigyan ka ng pagkakataon. = *You were given a chance. (Receiver of the action)*

SECOND PERSON PRONOUNS (PLURAL)

In English, we use the same word to indicate the plural *you*. In Tagalog, it is expressed by multiple pronouns.

First is **kayo** which is used as a subject and doer/receiver of the action.

Examples:
Lahat kayo ay magagaling. = *You are all amazing. (Subject)*
Nagpunta kayo sa Maynila kahapon. = *You went to Manila yesterday. (Doer of the action)*
Sinubukan naming intindihin kayo. = *We tried to understand you. (Receiver of the action)*

Ninyo and **inyo** are used to indicate possession, as in *your* and *yours* in plural form. **Ninyo** could also mean *you* as the doer of the action, but can never be a subject of a Tagalog sentence. **Inyo** can also act as a beneficiary of an action.

Examples:
Napakaganda ng bahay ninyo. = *Your house is very beautiful. (Possessive)*
Inyo ba ang gusaling iyon? = *Is that building yours? (Possessive)*

Niligpit ba ninyo ang mesa? = *Did you clear the table? (Doer of the action)*
Mga bata, ibibigay ko na ang regalo sa inyo. = *Kids, I'm going to give you the presents now. (Beneficiary of the action)*

One thing to note about these second person plural pronouns is that they are also used to politely address the person you are talking to. It is imperative that you use **kayo/ninyo/inyo** when referring to someone older than you, even if it's just one person.

Examples:
Kumain na po kayo? = *Did you already eat? (Polite)*
Kayo po ba ang nanay ni Marie? = *Are you the mother of Marie? (Polite)*
Lola, tinawag po ninyo ako? = *Grandma, did you call me? (Polite)*

> You can't use the singular pronouns, as in "**Kumain ka na?**" or "**Lola, tinawag mo ba ako?**" to address someone older, because it is considered rude.

THIRD PERSON PRONOUNS (SINGULAR)

Third person pronouns are those that refer to people outside of the conversation. In English, these pronouns are *he, she, they, them*, etc. In Tagalog, third person singular pronouns do not have any gender.

Siya is equivalent to *he/she* and *him/her*. It is used as the subject and doer/beneficiary of the action.

Examples:
Siya ay matalino. = *He/She is smart. (Subject)*
Nanonood siya ng telebisyon. = *He/She is watching the television. (Doer of the action)*
Inimbita ko siya sa bahay. = *I invited him/her to my house. (Beneficiary of the action)*

Niya and **kaniya** are used to indicate possession, as in *his/her* and *his/hers*. **Niya** could also mean *he/she* as the doer of the action, but can never be a subject of a Tagalog sentence. **Kaniya** can also act as a beneficiary of an action.

Examples:
Malinis ang kwarto niya. = *His/Her room is clean. (Possessive)*
Ang kwarto ay kaniya. = *The room is his/hers. (Possessive)*

Binigay niya ang pera sa akin. = *He/She gave the money to me. (Doer of the action)*
Binigay ko ang pera sa kaniya. = *I gave the money to him/her. (Beneficiary of the action)*

THIRD PERSON PRONOUNS (PLURAL)

Sila is used as a subject and object pronoun, as in *they/them*.

Examples:
Sila ay mayaman. = *They are rich. (Subject)*
Nag-aaral sila ng Mandarin. = *They are studying Mandarin. (Doer of the action)*
Gusto ko sila makita. = *I want to see them. (Receiver of the action)*

Nila and **kanila** are used to indicate possession, as in *their* and *theirs*. **Nila** could also mean *they* as the doer of the action, but can never be a subject of a Tagalog sentence. **Kanila** can also act as a beneficiary of an action.

Examples:
Bumaba ako ng kotse nila. = *I got out of their car. (Possessive)*
Kanila ang kotse. = *The car is theirs. (Possessive)*

Hinatid nila ako sa opisina. = *They dropped me off at the office. (Doer of the action)*
Ibinigay ko sa kanila ang susi. = *I gave the key to them. (Beneficiary of the action)*

THE ITO PRONOUN

The pronoun **ito** is used to refer to a thing in Tagalog. However, proximity plays a huge role when pertaining to things in Tagalog. Instead of *it*, *this* and *that* are more commonly used:

ito	*it/this (close to the speaker)*
iyan	*that (a little far from the speaker, nearer to the addressee)*
iyon	*that (far from both the speaker and addressee)*

Examples:
Hindi ko ito gusto. = *I don't like it/this.*
Gusto ko iyon. = *I want that.*
Pakipasa sa akin iyan. = *Please pass that to me.*

 **EXERCISE #2**

Punan ang patlang ng tamang panghalip.
Fill in the blanks with the right pronoun.

1. Pumunta _____ sa palengke. **(sila, kaniya, siya)**
   He/She went to the market.

2. Kinuha ni John ang pitaka _____. **(ko, iyo, ikaw)**
   John took my wallet.

3. _____ ay umalis na. **(Ito, Sila, Kami)**
   They already left.

4. Hihintayin _____. **(kita, octor, sila)**
   I will wait for you.

5. _____ po ba si Gng. Suarez? **(Ka, Siya, Kayo)**
   Are you Mrs. Suarez? (Polite)

6. Ang bisikletang ito ay _____. **(akin, iyon, ako)**
   This bicycle is mine.

7. Kainin mo ang pagkain _____. **(tayo, kanila, mo)**
   Eat your food.

8. Ang resort na ito ay _____. **(iyo, kaniya, nila)**
   This resort is his/hers.

9. Bumili _____ ng isda. **(kayo, kami, ikaw)**
   We bought fish.

10. Pakibuhat mo _____. **(ito, iyon, mo)**
    Please carry this.

 **LISTENING #1**

Makinig sa mga pahayag at isulat kung ano ang hinihingi.
Listen to the recording and write what is being asked.

1. _____
2. _____
3. _____
4. _____
5. _____
6. _____
7. _____
8. _____
9. _____
10. _____

B. VOCABULARY

Now that you already know your (polite) greetings and pronouns, it's time to level up your self-introduction by learning to describe your nationality, occupation, age, hobbies, family and even your moods. You will also be introduced to various question words in this vocabulary section.

NATIONALITY AND HOMETOWN

To express nationalities, you can say:

Ako ay <u>Pilipino</u>. (*I am a <u>Filipino</u>.*)

Tayo/Kami ay _____. (*We are _____.*)

Sila ay _____. (*They are _____.*)

Pilipino – *Filipino*	**Espanyol** – *Spanish*	**Portugis** – *Portuguese*
Amerikano – *American*	**Italyano** – *Italian*	**Kolumbyano** – *Colombian*
Hapon – *Japanese*	**Pranses** – *French*	**Ingles** – *English*
Koreyano – *Korean*	**Meksikano/Mehikano** – *Mexican*	**Aleman** – *German*
Tsino – *Chinese*	**Awstralyano** – *Australian*	**Aprikano** – *African*
Indyano – *Indian*	**Brasilyano** – *Brazilian*	**Arhentino** – *Argentinian*

You may also encounter native speakers who would introduce themselves as someone from a certain city or province in the Philippines:

Manilenyo – *from Manila*	**Ilonggo** – *from Iloilo*
Bulakenyo – *from Bulacan*	**Ilokano** – *from Ilocos*
Cebuano – *from Cebu*	**Masbatenyo** – *from Masbate*
Dabawenyo – *from Davao*	**Bisaya** – *from Visayas*

To express your home country, use the word **taga-** plus the name of your country.

Examples:
Ako ay taga-Amerika. = *I am from the United States.*
Siya ay taga-Pransya. = *He/She is from France.*
Kami ay taga-Pilipinas. = *We are from the Philippines.*

COMMON COUNTRIES/CONTINENTS:

Pilipinas – *Philippines*
Europa – *Europe*
Asya – *Asia*
Amerika – *America*
Italya – *Italy*
Espanya – *Spain*
Tsina – *China*

Awstralya – *Australia*
Koreya – *Korea*
Hapon – *Japan*
Brasil – *Brazil*
Portugal – *Portugal*
Singapura – *Singapore*
Inglatera – *England*

AGE

Next, let's talk about your age. When expressing your age, you can say:

Ako ay _____ taong gulang.   *(I am _____ years old.)*

Examples:
Ako ay dalawampung taong gulang.   *(I am twenty years old.)*
Ako ay labing-anim na taong gulang.   *(I am sixteen years old.)*

As mentioned, saying numerical expressions in full Tagalog may sound too formal for most native speakers. In normal conversations, age is expressed in either English or Spanish.

Examples:
Twenty-five years old na ako.   *(I am already twenty-five years old.)*
Magsi-sixty na siya.   *(He/She is turning sixty.)*

Si ate ay trenta anyos na.   *(My sister is thirty years old already.)*
Dose anyos pa lamang ang bata.   *(The child is just twelve years old.)*

OCCUPATION

Another vital part of your self-introduction is describing your work. Just like with nationality and age, you can introduce your work by saying **Ako ay _____**.

Examples:
Ako ay mananahi.   *(I am a tailor/dressmaker.)*
Ako ay doktor.   *(I am a doctor.)*
Ako ay drayber.   *(I am a driver.)*

If you want to sound more comprehensive/formal, you can add the word *isang* which literally means 'one'. In this context, **isang** acts as the article 'a', as in **isang doktor** = <u>*a* doctor</u>.

Examples:
Ako ay isang guro. *(I am a teacher.)*
Siya ay isang manunulat. *(He/She is a writer.)*

COMMON OCCUPATIONS

guro – *teacher*
manunulat – *writer*
doktor – *doctor*
mangingisda – *fisherman*
magsasaka – *farmer*
mang-aawit – *singer*
mananayaw – *dancer*
negosyante – *entrepreneur*

inhinyero – *engineer*
abogado – *lawyer*
mananahi/sastre – *tailor*
drayber – *driver*
gwardya – *security guard*
kasambahay – *maid*
mananaliksik – *researcher*
artista – *celebrity*

pintor – *painter*
mekaniko – *mechanic*
nars – *nurse*
bumbero – *fireman*
pulis – *police*
piloto – *pilot*
alahero – *jeweler*
hardinero – *gardener*

FAMILY

There are various expressions that you can use to introduce your family:

Galing ako sa <u>maliit na/malaking pamilya</u>. *(I am from a <u>small/big family</u>.)*
Mayroon akong <u>limang kapatid</u>. *(I have <u>five siblings</u>.)*
Mayroon akong <u>tatlong anak</u>. *(I have <u>three children</u>.)*
Ako ay <u>bunso</u>. *(I am the <u>youngest</u>.)*
Ako ay <u>panganay</u>. *(I am the <u>eldest</u>.)*
Ako ay <u>gitnang anak</u>. *(I am the <u>middle child</u>.)*

OTHER FAMILY-RELATED VOCABULARY

pamilya – *family*
kamag-anak – *relative*
magulang – *parent*
kapatid – *sibling*
anak – *child*
nanay – *mother*
tatay – *father*

ate – *older sister*
kuya – *older brother*
pinsan – *cousin*
tita – *aunt*
tito – *uncle*
lolo – *grandfather*
lola – *grandmother*

asawa – *spouse*
ninang – *godmother*
ninong – *godfather*
byenan – *mother/father-in-law*
manugang – *child-in-law*
ampon – *adopted*

HOBBIES

Of course, a self-introduction is not complete without talking about your hobbies. The easiest way to introduce your hobby is by using the phrase "**mahilig ako**" or which means *I love + verb*.

Examples:

Mahilig ako <u>kumanta</u>. (*I love to <u>sing</u>.*)
Mahilig siya <u>magluto</u>. (*He/She loves to cook.*)

You can also use the phrase "**paborito ko ang**" which means _____ *is my favorite*.

Examples:

Paborito ko ang pagsasayaw. (*Dancing is my favorite.*)
Paborito ko ang pagpinta. (*Painting is my favorite.*)
Paborito ko ang pagsusulat. (*Writing is my favorite.*)

COMMON HOBBIES

paglangoy – *swimming*
pagtakbo – *running*
pagbabasa – *reading*
pagtugtog ng gitara – *playing the guitar*
pagtugtog ng piano – *playing the piano*
paglalaro – *gaming/playing*
pananahi – *sewing*
panonood – *watching*

pangingisda – *fishing*
pangangabayo – *horseback riding*
pag-akyat ng bundok – *hiking*
pagmamaneho – *driving*
paglalakad – *walking*
pangongolekta – *collecting*
paglalakbay – *traveling*
pakikinig sa musika – *listening to music*

MOODS OR EMOTIONS

Whether you're excited or disappointed, it's important that you are able to express your emotions too. In Tagalog, you can just say "**Ako ay** _____" which means *I am/feel* _____.

Examples:

Ako ay masaya. (*I am happy.*)
Ako ay malungkot. (*I feel sad.*)
Ako ay takot. (*I am scared.*)
Ako ay nagtataka. (*I am wondering*)

COMMON MOODS AND FEELINGS

galit – *angry*
nagtatampo – *holding a grudge*
nagulat – *surprised*
bagot – *bored*
sabik – *excited*
kabado – *nervous*
nagagalak – *joyful*
nagpapasalamat – *thankful*
nahihiya – *shy*
naguguluhan – *confused*
inaantok – *sleepy*
buhay na buhay – *lively*
may tiwala sa sarili – *confident*
masayang masaya – *ecstatic*
komportable – *comfortable*
hindi komportable – *uncomfortable*
manhid – *numb*
ganado – *energized*
namamangha – *amused*
kalmado – *calm*

EXERCISE #3

A. Tukuyin ang mga bansang sinasagisag ng bawat bandila.
Identify the country based on the flag.

1.

2.

3.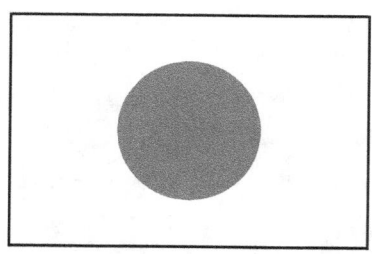

4.

5.

6.

7.

8.

B. Isalin ang mga sumusunod na pangungusap sa Tagalog. Gamitin ang mga halimbawa bilang gabay.

Translate the following sentences to Tagalog. Use the examples as your guide.

> Ex. I am a fisherman. = **Ako ay mangingisda.**
> I love to dance. = **Mahilig ako sumayaw.**
> Traveling is my favorite. = **Paborito ko ang pamamasyal.**
> He/She is thirty years old. = **Siya ay tatlumpung taong gulang.**

1. *I am a teacher.* _____
2. *He/She is a doctor.* _____
3. *I love to cook.* _____
4. *He/She loves to sing.* _____
5. *I am a lawyer.* _____
6. *I am the youngest.* _____
7. *I am from a big family.* _____
8. *Fishing is my favorite.* _____
9. *Hiking is his/her favorite.* _____
10. *I am twenty years old.* _____

C. Piliin ang iyong magiging damdamin sa mga sumusunod na pahayag.

Choose the emotion that you will feel from the following statements.

masaya   malungkot   galit   nagulat

_____ 1. "Hindi na kita mahal." *("I don't love you anymore.")*

_____ 2. "Ninakaw ko ang pera mo." *("I stole your money.")*

_____ 3. "Nanalo ka sa Lotto!" *("You won the lottery!")*

_____ 4. "May sakit ang nanay mo." *("Your mom is sick.")*

_____ 5. "Mahal kita!" *("I love you!")*

_____ 6. "Hindi ka tanggap sa trabaho." *("You didn't get the job.")*

_____ 7. "May sunog!" *("There's fire!")*

_____ 8. "Ipinagmamalaki kita." *("I am proud of you.")*

_____ 9. "Wala kang kwenta." *("You are worthless.")*

_____ 10. "Niloko kita." *("I cheated on you.")*

ASKING QUESTIONS

The last part of Section 2 deals with forming questions. The two types of questions in Tagalog are the Yes-No questions and the WH-questions.

Yes-No questions in Tagalog are formed with the question marker **ba**. It is usually inserted after the subject/predicate but never at beginning of the sentence.

Examples:

Question 1
Pupunta ka ba sa simbahan? = *Are you going to the church?*

Answer 1
Oo, pupunta ako sa simbahan. = *Yes, I am going to the church.*
Hindi, hindi ako pupunta sa simbahan. = *No, I am not going to the church.*

Question 2
Ikaw ba ang aplikante? = *Are you the applicant?*

Answer 2
Oo, ako ang aplikante. = *Yes, I am the applicant.*
Hindi, hindi ako ang aplikante. = *No, I am not the applicant.*

Question 3
Umuulan ba? = *Is it raining?*

Answer 3
Oo, umuulan. = *Yes, it's raining.*
Hindi, hindi umuulan. = *No, it's not raining.*

Question 4
Nakakatakot ba ang palabas? = *Is the show scary?*

Answer 4
Oo, nakakatakot ang palabas. = *Yes, the show is scary.*
Hindi, hindi nakakatakot ang palabas. = *No, the show is not scary.*

To form WH-questions, here is the table of the words that you need to remember:

ENGLISH	TAGALOG
What	Ano
Who	Sino
Where	Saan
Why	Bakit
When	Kailan
Which	Alin
How	Paano
How	Kumusta (condition or state)
How much	Magkano (price) Gaano (measurement)
How many	Ilan
Whom/Whose	Kanino
With whom	Na kanino (possession)

Just like in English, these WH-markers in Tagalog are usually found at the beginning of the sentence.

Examples:

Ano ang kinain mo kagabi?   (*What* did you eat last night?)
Sino ang nagsara ng pinto?   (*Who* closed the door?)
Saan ka bumili ng gulay?   (*Where* did you buy the vegetables?)
Bakit siya nandito?   (*Why* is he/she here?)
Kailan ka aalis papuntang Amerika?   (*When* are you leaving for the US?)
Alin sa dalawang damit ang pinili mo?   (*Which* of the two clothes did you choose?)
Paano ko lulutuin ang manok?   (*How* will I cook the chicken?) (method)
Kumusta ang pagkain mo?   (*How* is your food?) (state/condition)
Magkano ang mga sapatos na ito?   (*How much* are these shoes?) (price)
Gaano kabigat ang timbang mo?   (*How* much do you weigh?) (measurement)

Ilan ang gusto mo? (*How many* do you want?)
Kanino ang sulat na ito? (*Whose* letter is this?)
Kanino mo binigay ang bayad? (*To whom* did you give the payment?)
Na kanino ang susi? (*With whom* are the keys?)

In Tagalog, some of these WH-markers are reduplicated to express plurality.

Examples:

Saan-saan ka na nakapaglakbay? (*Which places* have you traveled to?)
Anu-ano ang mga pinamili mo? (*What are the things* that you bought?)
Kani-kanino ang mga gamit na ito? (*Who are the owners* of these things?)

 **EXERCISE #4**

Piliin ang pinakaangkop na salitang-pangkatanungan upang makumpleto ang pangungusap.
Choose the correct question word to complete the sentence.

Saan	Alin
Ano	Kailan
Bakit	Magkano
Sino	Paano
Kanino	Kumusta

1. _____ ang pumirma sa dokumentong ito?
   (Who signed this document?)

2. _____ ka nakatira?
   (Where do you live?)

3. _____ ang kailangan kong ipunin para sa kompyuter?
   (How much money do I need to save for the computer?)

4. _____ ka makakarating sa Maynila?
   (How will you get to Manila?)

5. _____ ang pag-aaral mo?
   (How are your studies?)

6. _____ ka magdidiwang ng iyong kaarawan?
   (When are you going to celebrate your birthday?)

7. _____ ang mas gusto mo, itong sapatos o itong relo?
   (Which one do you like more, these shoes or this watch?)

8. _____ iyang jaket na suot mo?
   (Whose jacket are you wearing?)

9. _____ ka umiiyak?
   (Why are you crying?)

10. _____ ang gusto mo paglaki mo?
    (What do you want to be when you grow up?)

LISTENING #2

Makinig sa pagpapakilala ni Mark Abella sa unang araw ng klase at sagutin ang mga tanong.
Listen to Mark Abella's self-introduction on the first day of class and answer the questions.

_____ 1. What is the teacher's name?

_____ 2. As Mark is a native speaker of the Tagalog language, what city or province did he come from?

_____ 3. As he is a native speaker of the Tagalog language, what city or province did Mark's father come from?

_____ 4. What is the occupation of Mark's mother?

_____ 5. How many siblings does Mark have?

_____ 6. How old is Mark?

_____ 7. If Mark has extra money / budget, what does he want to do?

_____ 8. What is the occupation of Mark's father?

_____ 9. What does Mark feel as a newcomer in the class?

_____ 10. What mood of Mark's can help him make new friends?

SECTION 3

GAANO MO KAKILALA ANG IYONG SARILI?
HOW WELL DO YOU KNOW YOURSELF?

This section is all about describing yourself in much more depth. You will learn to detail your physical traits, your preferences, and your personality. The grammar part deals with articles, noun pluralization, degrees of adjectives, and negation. For the vocabulary, you will learn to express basic descriptions. From describing your body parts to talking about your passions, your self-introduction just keeps getting better and better!

A. GRAMMAR

ARTICLES

Just like English, Tagalog also uses several articles to introduce a noun phrase. These articles are **ang**, **ng**, **si** and **sina**. **Ang** is closest to the definite article *the*, while **ng** equates to *a* or *an*. Be careful not to confuse it with the other **ng** though, which functions as the prepositions *of* and *by*. This will be discussed in the next chapters.

Examples:
Gusto ko ng pusa. = *I want a cat.*
Gusto ko ang pusa. = *I want the cat.*
✗ Gusto ko ang pusa **ng** kaibigan ko. = *I want the cat of my friend.*

Binigyan ko si Maricris ng relo. = *I gave Maricris a watch.*
Ibinigay ko ang relo kay Maricris. = *I gave Maricris the watch.*
✗ Ibinigay ko ang relo **ng** tatay ko kay Maricris. = *I gave the watch of my father to Maricris.*

Kumain kami ng mansanas. = *We ate an apple.*
Kinain namin ang mansanas. = *We ate the apple.*
✗ Ang mansanas ay kinuha **ng** anak mo. = *The apple was taken by your child.*

It is important to note that in Tagalog, **ng**, as an indefinite article, is only used if it is the direct object of the verb in the sentence. It cannot stand alone in any other case and would simply be omitted. On the other hand, the definite article **ang** is used in any context.

Examples:
She is a doctor. → **Siya ay doktor.** *(literal: She is doctor.)*
She is the doctor. → **Siya (ay) ang doktor.** *(In this case, the linking verb 'ay' is usually omitted.)*

I am not a liar. → **Hindi ako sinungaling.** *(literal: I am not liar.)*
I am not the liar. → **Hindi ako ang sinungaling.**

AS ANSWERS TO QUESTIONS

What did you eat? A banana. → **Ano ang kinain mo? Saging.**
What did you eat? The banana. → **Ano ang kinain mo? Ang saging.**

What do you want? A computer. → **Ano ang gusto mo? Kompyuter.**
What do you want? The computer. → **Ano ang gusto mo? Ang kompyuter.**

Tagalog also uses separate articles to refer to people. These are **si** (*singular*) and **sina/sila** (*plural*).

Examples:
Si Amanda ay maganda. = *Amanda is beautiful.*
Pumunta si nanay sa palengke. = *Mama went to the market.*

Sina/sila Jose at Wally ang sumundo sa akin. = *I was picked up by Jose and Wally.*
Bumisita sina/sila tatay sa bahay ko. = *Papa (and company) visited my house.*

Remember that **si** and **sina/sila** can only be used for proper pronouns or specific names/people. It cannot be used to refer to a common noun, as in teacher (***X si*** guro) or police (***X si*** pulis).

THE DEMONSTRATIVE PRONOUN 'YUNG

From the word **iyong** which means demonstrative *that*, **'yung** is commonly used by Tagalog native speakers as a definite article in informal conversations. Literally translating to *that* + noun, **'yung** actually stands as *the* + noun in this context. This can be used for both things and people.

Examples:
Kinuha ko 'yung pera sa ibabaw ng mesa. = *I took the money on top of the table.*
Nakakatakot 'yung pelikula. = *The movie was scary.*
Kinausap ko 'yung nanay ni John. = *I talked to the mom of John.*

EXERCISE #1

Isulat ang tamang pantukoy para sa mga sumusunod na pangngalan.
Write the correct article for the following nouns.

1. *the dog* = _____ **aso**

2. *John* = _____ **John**

3. *an airplane* = _____ **eroplano** (*object*)

4. *the church* = _____ **simbahan**

5. *the doctor* = _____ **doktor** (*informal the*)

6. *Steve and Jake* = _____ **Steve at Jake**

7. *Papa* = _____ **Papa**

8. *the class* = _____ **klase** (*informal the*)

9. *a gift* = _____ **regalo** (*object*)

10. *the shoes* = _____ **mga sapatos**

NOUN PLURALIZATION

The plurality of Tagalog nouns is marked by the word **mga** (pronounced as ma-NGA) + noun.

Examples:
mga problema = *problems*
mga kaibigan = *friends*
ang mga bahay = *the houses*
ang mga bata = *the children*

Nagpunta ang mga pulis dito. = *The policemen came here.*
Ang mga aso ay tumatakbo. = *The dogs are running.*
Binigyan ko ng ilang mga damit si Teresa. = *I gave Teresa some clothes.*

Another way of indicating noun plurality in Tagalog is by partial or full reduplication of the word. These reduplicated words can stand alone or can still be used after the word **mga**.

(Note that reduplicated plural nouns are only used in certain contexts by native speakers. The most common way to express plurality in Tagalog is still **mga** + noun.)

Examples:
mga anak → **(mga) anak-anak** = *children*
mga supot → **(mga) supot-supot** = *plastic bags*
mga tonelada → **(mga) tone-tonelada** = *tons*

Isinali namin ang mga anak-anak namin sa kompetisyon. = *We entered our children in the competition.*
Sako-sakong bigas ang dumating kahapon. = *Sacks of rice arrived yesterday.*
Bumili ako ng kahon-kahon na gatas. = *I bought cartons of milk.*

PLURAL NOUNS + ADJECTIVES

Partial reduplication also occurs in Tagalog adjectives that modify plural nouns.

Examples:
beautiful = **maganda** → **magaganda**
smart = **matalino** → **matatalino**
arrogant = **mayabang** → **mayayabang**

Maganda ang larawan. = *The picture is beautiful.*
Magaganda ang mga larawan. = *The pictures are beautiful.*

Matalino ang bata. = *The kid is smart.*
Matatalino ang mga bata. = *The kids are smart.*

Mayabang si Jeff. = *Jeff is arrogant.*
Mayayabang sina Jeff at mga kaibigan niya. = *Jeff and his friends are arrogant.*

PLURAL NOUNS + VERBS

For Tagalog verbs with plural actors, the prefix **nagsi-** is added to the verb.

Examples:
ran = **tumakbo** → **nagsitakbo**
eating = **kumakain** → **nagsisikain**
sang = **kumanta** → **nagsikantahan**

Nagsitakbo ang mga aso dahil sa takot. = *The dogs ran away because of fear.*
Ang mga bata ay **nagsisikain** ng hapunan. = *The children are eating dinner.*
Nagsikantahan ang mga ibon. = *The birds sang.*

DEGREES OF ADJECTIVES

Tagalog adjectives are usually formed by adding the prefix **ma-** to nouns, as in:

ma + ganda (*beauty*) = **maganda** (*beautiful*)
ma + init (*heat*) = **mainit** (*hot*)
ma + dilim (*darkness*) = **madilim** (*dark*)

Now, how do we form adjectival phrases or adjective + noun?

We use ligatures. Ligatures are particles that connect the modifier to the word that it modifies. In Tagalog, these ligatures equate to '*that*', as in *the dog that is running* or *the child that is beautiful*.

Note that these ligatures are not only used for adjectives but across all words that need to be linked in Tagalog.

There are three ligatures in Tagalog:

-ng = a suffix attached to a word that ends in a vowel
-g = a suffix attached to a word that ends in the letter *n*
na = added after a word that ends in a consonant except the letter *n*; not an affix but a separate word

Examples:

maganda + babae → **magandang babae** = *beautiful girl (literal: a girl that is beautiful)*
mataba + aso → **matabang aso** = *fat dog (literal: a dog that is fat)*
mababa + grado → **mababang grado** = *low grade (literal: a grade that is low)*

huwaran + empleyado → **huwarang empleyado** = *model employee*
mamahalin + pinggan → **mamahaling pinggan** = *expensive plate*
katamtaman + temperatura → **katamtamang temperatura** = *moderate temperature*

manipis + tela → **manipis na tela** = *thin cloth*
mahirap + problema → **mahirap na problema** = *difficult problem*
maliit + pusa → **maliit na pusa** = *small cat*

COMPARING ADJECTIVES

Now that you know how to form basic adjectives and adjectival phrases, it's time to learn their comparative and superlative degrees.

In Tagalog, the word **mas** is used before an adjective to signify *more* while the prefix **pinaka-** is added to signify *most*.

Examples:

mas matangkad = *taller*
mas malambot = *softer*
mas masinop = *more organized*

pinakamabait = *kindest*
pinakamalalim = *deepest*
pinakamahal = *most expensive*

Even in their comparative and superlative forms, the modified noun still comes after the adjectives.

Examples:

pinakamagandang lugar = *most beautiful place*
mas payat na bata = *skinnier kid*
pinakamurang sapatos = *cheapest shoes*

Notice how there is no equivalent word for *less* or *least* in Tagalog. So, if you want to say phrases such as *less happy* or *least difficult*, you can just use **mas/pinaka-** + the opposite or negated form of the adjective.

Examples:

less happy = **mas malungkot** *(sadder)* or **mas hindi masaya** *(not happier)*

least difficult = **pinakamadali** *(easiest)* or **pinaka hindi mahirap** *(not the most difficult)*

As seen from the examples above, the affix **pinaka-** becomes a separate word when preceding **hindi**. We cannot connect the two words as in **pinakahindi**. This affix can only be attached to adjectives.

Another common way to express the idea of *less* in Tagalog is by saying **hindi gaano** or **hindi masyado** which literally translates to *not (too) much*.

Examples:

hindi gaanong mahal = *less expensive (literal: not too expensive)*
hindi masyadong maanghang = *less spicy (literal: not too spicy)*
hindi gaanong madaldal = *less talkative (literal: not too talkative)*

Now let's move on to forming complete sentences using your adjectives. For comparative and superlative degrees, the additional words that you'll need to remember are:

kaysa kay = *than (used for a specific name or person; singular)*
kaysa kina = *than (used for specific names or people; plural)*
kaysa sa = *than (used for the rest)*
sa lahat = *among all of them*

Here's a comparison table:

POSITIVE	COMPARATIVE	SUPERLATIVE
Si Maria ay maganda. Maria is beautiful.	Si Maria ay mas maganda kaysa kay Stephanie. Maria is more beautiful than Stephanie.	Si Maria ang pinakamaganda sa lahat ng babae dito. Maria is the most beautiful among all the women here.
Ang bata ay masaya. The child is happy.	Ang bata ay mas masaya kaysa sa kaniyang nanay. The child is happier than his/her mother.	Ang bata ang pinakamasaya sa lahat ng tao sa bahay. The child is the happiest among all the people in the house.
Masarap ang manok sa Jollibee. The chicken from Jollibee is delicious.	Mas masarap ang manok sa Jollibee kaysa sa McDonalds. The chicken from Jollibee is more delicious than McDonald's.	Pinakamasarap ang manok sa Jollibee sa lahat ng kainan sa Pilipinas. The chicken from Jollibee is the most delicious among all restaurants in the Philippines.

NEGATION

In the previous lessons, you have been introduced to the negation marker **hindi** in Tagalog. This word means *not* and its contracted form is **'di**. To negate a word or an expression in Tagalog, just put **hindi** or **'di** before the word or the subject/predicate.

Examples:

NEGATING NOUNS

hindi lalaki = *not a man*
hindi pusa = *not a cat*
'di salamin = *not a mirror*

NEGATING ADJECTIVES

hindi malinaw = *not clear*
hindi matapang = *not brave*
'di malamig = *not cold*

NEGATING ADVERBS

hindi sa loob = *not inside*
hindi kahapon = *not yesterday*
'di marahan = *not gently*

NEGATING VERBS

hindi kumain = *did not eat*
hindi nagsasayaw = *does not dance*
'di magsasalita = *will not speak*

OTHER TYPES OF NEGATION

Aside from *not*, negation can also be in the form of *no*, *nothing* and *don't*. So, how do we express them in Tagalog? The two words that you need to remember are:

wala = *no, nothing*
huwag/'wag = *do not/don't*

The positioning of these negation markers is the same as **hindi**. They are used before the word they modify.

Examples:

walang pera = *no money*
walang trabaho = *no job*
walang pamilya = *no family*

huwag matakot = *do not be afraid*
huwag magnakaw = *do not steal*
'wag mag-away = *don't fight*

When it comes to negating an entire sentence, the position of your markers will depend on the sentence pattern that you used. If you're using the active voice, for example with the linking verb **ay**, the negation marker precedes the word it modifies. Otherwise, it is found at the initial position of the sentence.

Examples:

Ako ay hindi masaya. = *I am not happy.*
Hindi ako masaya. = *I am not happy.*

Si Alvin ay hindi nag-aaral. = *Alvin is not studying.*
Hindi nag-aaral si Alvin. = *Alvin is not studying.*

Ako ay <u>wala</u>ng kasalanan. = I have <u>no</u> fault.
<u>Wala</u> akong kasalanan. = I have <u>no</u> fault.

Sina May at Oliver ay <u>wala</u>ng kinatatakutan. = May and Oliver fear <u>no</u> one.
<u>Wala</u>ng kinatatakutan sina May at Oliver. = May and Oliver fear <u>no</u> one.

Ikaw ay <u>huwag</u> magsisinungaling. = <u>Do not</u> lie.
<u>Huwag</u> kang magsisinungaling. = <u>Do not</u> lie.

Ikaw ay '<u>wag</u> magiging mayabang. = <u>Don't</u> become arrogant.
'<u>Wag</u> kang magiging mayabang. = <u>Don't</u> become arrogant.

EXERCISE #2

Isalin ang mga sumusunod na parirala.
Translate the following phrases.

1. *not happy* = _____
2. *more beautiful than Jennie* = _____
3. *matabang aso* = _____
4. *don't study* = _____
5. *no money* = _____
6. *walang doktor* = _____
7. *pinakamabait* = _____
8. *hottest* = _____
9. *mas masarap* = _____
10. *do not speak* = _____

LISTENING #1

Makinig nang mabuti at sagutin ang mga tanong.
Listen carefully and answer the questions.

_____ 1. What word did the speaker use to describe the gifts received?

_____ 2. What gift did the mother give?

_____ 3. Who came to the speaker's house?

_____ 4-5. What gifts did the friends give?

_____ 6-8. What fruits did the speaker serve?

_____ 9. What attitude do the friends have that makes the party so much fun?

_____ 10. How did the speaker describe this year's birthday?

B. VOCABULARY

Now that you know how to form adjectives and even compare them, it's time to jump right into describing yourself!

PHYSICAL TRAITS

Just like expressing your nationality or your occupation, describing your physical traits also follows the pattern **Ako ay** _____. Before we delve into the different adjectives you can use, let's start with the body parts that you can describe first:

ulo – head
kamay – hand
paa – foot
binti – leg
hita – thigh
daliri – finger
palad – palm
balat – skin
buhok – hair
kuko – nail
braso – arm
tiyan – belly

mata – eye
kilay – eyebrow
ilong – nose
noo – forehead
tainga/tenga – ear
pisngi – cheek
ngipin – tooth
bibig – mouth
labi – lips
mukha – face
katawan – body
balakang – hips

To describe your body parts, you can say:

Ako ay may _____. = I have _____.

Ako ay may <u>itim na buhok</u>. = I have <u>black hair</u>.

Ako ay may <u>matangos na ilong</u>. = I have a <u>pointed nose</u>.

Ako ay may <u>matabang pisngi</u>. = I have <u>chubby cheeks</u>.

Ako ay may <u>maputlang balat</u>. = I have <u>pale skin</u>.

Ako ay may <u>payat na katawan</u>. = I have a <u>skinny body</u>.

Ako ay may <u>maliit na kamay</u>. = I have <u>small hands</u>.

Ako may <u>makapal na labi</u>. = I have <u>thick lips</u>.

OTHER ADJECTIVES TO DESCRIBE YOUR PHYSICAL TRAITS

matangkad – *tall*
pandak – *short*
mataba – *fat*
payat – *thin/skinny*
matanda – *old*
bata – *young*
maganda – *pretty*
gwapo/pogi – *handsome*
maitim/morena/moreno – *brown-skinned*
maputi – *fair-skinned*

malaki – *huge*
maliit – *tiny*
mahaba ang buhok – *long-haired*
maiksi ang buhok – *short-haired*
maporma – *stylish*
malakas ang dating – *strong aura/appeal*
mabigat – *heavy*
magaan – *light*
malakas – *physically strong*
mahina/lampa – *physically weak*

OTHER ADJECTIVES TO DESCRIBE THE PHYSICAL TRAITS OF OBJECTS

magaspang – *rough*
makinis – *smooth*
manipis – *thin*
makapal – *thick*
malabo – *blurred*
makinang – *shiny*
malinis – *clean*
madumi – *dirty*
matulis – *sharp*
mapurol – *dull*
bago – *new*
luma – *old*
makulay – *colorful*
mabango – *good-smelling*
mabaho – *bad-smelling*

mahaba – *long*
maiksi – *short*
bilugan – *round*
kwadrado – *squared*
matigas – *hard*
malambot – *soft*
malutong – *crispy*
makunat – *chewy*
mataas – *high*
mababa – *low*
malaki – *big*
maliit – *small*
matibay – *sturdy*

Aside from the (**Ako ay** *(adjective)* or **Si/Ang** *(subject)* **ay** *(adjective).*) pattern, you can also say the adjective first, then the subject, as in *[(Adjective)* **ako** or *(Adjective)* **si/ang** *(subject).].*

Examples:

Ako ay pandak. = I am short.
Pandak ako. = I am short.

Si Shane ay maputi. = *Shane is <u>fair-skinned</u>.*
Maputi si Shane. = *Shane is <u>fair-skinned</u>.*

Ang tatay ko ay gwapo. = *My father is <u>handsome</u>.*
Gwapo ang tatay ko. = *My father is <u>handsome</u>.*

Ang kumot ay madumi. = *The blanket is <u>dirty</u>.*
Madumi ang kumot. = *The blanket is <u>dirty</u>.*

Ang upuan ay matibay. = *The chair is <u>sturdy</u>.*
Matibay ang upuan. = *The chair is <u>sturdy</u>.*

EXERCISE #3

A. Pagtugmain ang mga sumusunod.
Match the following.

| A. labi | C. paa | E. braso | G. ilong | I. binti |
| B. buhok | D. kamay | F. ulo | H. tainga | J. mata |

 1. _____

 6. _____

 2. _____

 7. _____

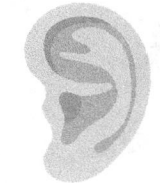 3. _____

 8. _____

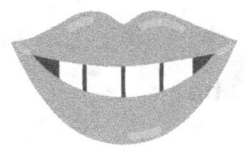 4. _____

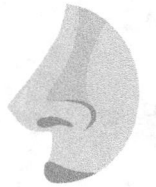 9. _____

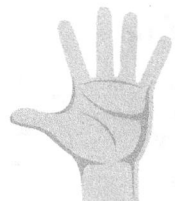 5. _____

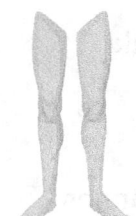 10. _____

B. Piliin ang angkop na pang-uri sa mga sumusunod na salita.
Choose the correct adjective for the following words.

1. bato *(rock)*

   a. mahina	b. malakas	c. matigas

2. buhok *(hair)*

   a. matangkad	b. mahaba	c. lampa

3. mukha *(face)*

   a. bilugan	b. makulay	c. mapurol

4. mesa *(table)*

   a. masarap	b. luma	c. malutong

5. balat *(skin)*

   a. morena	b. makinang	c. mataas

6. damit *(clothes)*

   a. mataba	b. makapal	c. pandak

7. kutsilyo *(knife)*

   a. matangos	b. matangkad	c. matulis

8. daliri *(finger)*

   a. bago	b. maiksi	c. malabo

9. tiyan *(belly)*

   a. malaki	b. masarap	c. maporma

10. kutson *(mattress)*

    a. matangos	b. malambot	c. gwapo

PERSONALITY

In Section 2, you learned how to express your emotions or disposition, such as being nervous or excited. But what if someone asks you, *"What kind of person are you?"* It's important that you are armed with different adjectives to describe your personality to them!

COMMON PERSONALITY DESCRIPTIONS

malikhain – *creative*
madiskarte – *resourceful*
mapagmahal – *loving*
pasensyoso/pasensyosa – *patient*
mapagbigay – *generous*
mapagkumbaba – *humble*
nakakatawa – *funny*
masayahin – *cheerful*
mahiyain – *shy*
tahimik – *quiet*
mainitin ang ulo – *hot-headed*

kuripot – *stingy*
masikap – *persevering*
masipag – *hardworking*
nakakainis – *annoying*
madaling kausap – *easy to deal with*
strikto – *strict*
palakaibigan – *friendly*
pursigido – *determined*
magalang – *polite*
sensitibo – *sensitive*
mapagparaya – *selfless*

Examples:

<u>Masayahin</u> ako. = *I am <u>cheerful</u>.*
Ako ay <u>pasensyoso</u>. = *I am <u>patient</u>.* – male; **pasensyosa** *is used for female speakers*
<u>Madiskarte</u> ang magulang ko. = *My parents are <u>resourceful</u>.*
Si Jen ay <u>palakaibigan</u>. = *Jen is <u>friendly</u>.*
<u>Malikhain</u> ako. = *I am <u>creative</u>.*

 **EXERCISE #4**

Basahin ang mga sumusunod na sitwasyon at ibigay ang angkop na personalidad sa bawat karakter.
Read the following situations and give the most accurate personality trait for the character.

_____ 1. Mahilig magpatawa si Kevin.
 (Kevin loves making people laugh.)

_____ 2. Ayaw ni Jordan na ipagyabang ang kaniyang kayamanan.
 (Jordan doesn't like to brag about his wealth.)

_____ 3. Hindi mabilis magalit si Daniel.
 (Daniel doesn't get angry easily.)

_____ 4. Inuuna ni Karen ang ibang tao kaysa ang kaniyang sarili.
 (Karen puts other people before herself.)

_____ 5. Madalas magbahagi ng pagkain si Jake sa mga mahihirap.
 (Jake always shares food with the needy.)

_____ 6. Mabilis magkaroon ng bagong kaibigan si Donna.
 (Donna is quick to make new friends.)

_____ 7. Ayaw na ayaw ni Lee gastusin ang kaniyang pera kahit kailangan.
 (Even when it's necessary, Lee doesn't like spending his money.)

_____ 8. Parating nagsasabi ng *po* at *opo* ang anak ni Lou.
 (Lou's kid always uses po *and* opo*).*

_____ 9. Mabilis mainis si Eric.
 (Eric gets easily irritated/angry.)

_____ 10. Madalas humindi ang magulang ni Tricia pagdating sa paglabas-labas.
 (Tricia's parents usually say no when it comes to hanging out/going outside.)

PREFERENCES AND PASSIONS

Levelling up from sharing your hobbies, it's now time to talk about your favorites and passions. From your favorite color to the things that you're extremely passionate about, here are some vocabulary words that will surely help you talk about them.

COLORS

pula – *red*
asul – *blue*
dilaw – *yellow*
kahel – *orange*
itim – *black*
puti – *white*
kayumanggi – *brown*
berde – *green*
lila – *violet*
abo – *gray*
rosas – *pink*
ginto – *gold*
tanso – *bronze*
pilak – *silver*

FOOD/TASTE

maanghang – *spicy*
matamis – *sweet*
mapait – *bitter*
maalat – *salty*
maasim – *sour*
prutas – *fruit*
gulay – *vegetables*
kanin – *rice*
isda – *fish*
baboy – *pork*
baka – *beef*

manok – *chicken*
panghimagas – *dessert*
tsokolate – *chocolate*
kape – *coffee*
tsaa – *tea*
yelo – *ice*
biskwit – *biscuit*
meryenda – *snack*
sabaw – *soup*
prito – *fried*
inihaw – *grilled*

As you have learned from the previous sections, the phrases you can use to introduce your favorites are **Mahilig ako sa** (I am fond of) _____ or **Paborito ko ang** (My favorite is)_____.

Examples:
Mahilig ako sa kanin. = I am fond of rice.
Dilaw ang paborito kong kulay. = Yellow is my favorite color.
Mahilig akong uminom ng kape. = I am fond of drinking coffee.
Paborito ni nanay ang mga matatamis. = Sweets are Mom's favorite.
Paborito kong pagkain ang panghimagas. = My favorite food is dessert.

Now if you want to talk about your passions, you should use the expression **Gusto ko ang** (I like) _____ or **Mahal ko ang** (I love/I am passionate about) _____.

COMMON PASSIONS

pagtuturo – teaching
pag-akyat ng bundok – hiking
pagtulong sa kapwa – helping others
pagsusulat – writing
pagbabasa – reading
pag-arte – acting
pagkuha ng litrato – photography
pagkanta – singing
pagsayaw – dancing

pagguhit – drawing
pagluluto – cooking
paggawa ng musika – making music
paggigitara – playing the guitar
pagbibisikleta – cycling
pagsisid – diving
pag-aalaga ng bata – childcaring
pag-aalaga ng halaman – gardening
pagboboluntaryo – volunteering

Examples:

Mahal ko ang pagtuturo.	=	I love teaching.
Gusto ni ate ang pagluluto.	=	My sister likes cooking.
Mahal ko ang paggawa ng musika.	=	I love making music.
Gusto ni tatay ang pagbibisikleta.	=	My father likes cycling.
Mahal ng kaibigan ko ang pag-arte.	=	My friend loves acting.

EXERCISE #5

A. Piliin ang tamang kulay para sa mga sumusunod na bagay.
Choose the correct color for the following objects.

| dilaw | itim | asul | berde | pula |

1. araw *(sun)* = _____

2. dahon *(leaf)* = _____

3. dagat *(sea)* = _____

4. dugo *(blood)* = _____

5. buhok *(hair)* = _____

B. Piliin ang tamang salita na tumutugma sa mga larawan.
Choose the word that best matches the illustration.

A. pagbibisikleta
B. pagkuha ng litrato
C. pagkain ng matatamis
D. pag-inom ng tsaa
E. pagtulong sa kapwa
F. paggigitara
G. pagkanta
H. pagsusulat
I. pag-aalaga ng bata
J. pagtuturo

1. _____

6. _____

2. _____

3. _____

4. _____

5. _____

7. _____

8. _____

9. _____

10. _____

 **LISTENING #2**

Makinig nang mabuti at ibigay ang mga salitang naglalarawan sa mga bahagi ng katawan.
Listen carefully and identify the words used to describe the different parts of the body.

_____ 1. face

_____ 2. cheeks

_____ 3. skin

_____ 4. nose

_____ 5. hair

Makinig at isulat ang personalidad na binabanggit.
Listen and write the descriptions of personalities as mentioned in the recording.

_____ 6. Pedro as a student.

_____ 7. The trait of Pedro's mother.

_____ 8. The trait of Pedro's father.

_____ 9. Pedro's father as he performs his work.

_____ 10. Pedro's trait when he's using "po."

SECTION 4

KILALANIN MO RIN ANG IBA
GET TO KNOW OTHERS TOO

This section extends your knowledge from being able to introduce yourself to being able to relate to the people around you. You will learn to describe people and things using adjectives' degrees of description. The grammar part will also cover common noun affixes, demonstrative pronouns, and enclitic particles. On the other hand, your vocabulary will be enriched with terms that can express your personal relationships, from those inside your house to those in your community.

A. GRAMMAR

DEGREES OF DESCRIPTION

So, you have learned all about the adjectives' degrees of comparison *(more/less and most)*; now it's time to talk about their degrees of description. An adjective's degree of description refers to its intensity—such as being *too* beautiful or *a little* annoying. There are three degrees of description in Tagalog: **Lantay**, **Katamtaman** and **Masidhi**.

LANTAY (SIMPLE):

This degree of description refers to the basic or neutral form of the adjective. Examples are:

matalino – *smart*
masigla – *lively*
matanda – *old*

KATAMTAMAN (MODERATE)

These adjectives are accompanied by words that express the meaning of *somewhat*, *a little* or *slightly*. The word **medyo** is used before the adjective while **nang kaunti/nang bahagya** are used after the adjective.

Examples are:

medyo tahimik = *a little* quiet

medyo masungit = *a little* snobby

maingay **nang bahagya** = *a little* noisy

malungkot **nang kaunti** = *a little* sad

A partial/full reduplication of some adjectives may also occur to connote its moderate intensity. Examples are:

mahirap-hirap = *a little difficult*

maalat-alat = *a little salty*

mabilis-bilis = *a little quick*

madilim-dilim = *a little dark*

MASIDHI (SUPER)

The last degree of description is the most intense among the three. These adjectives are accompanied by words and prefixes that express the meanings of *very, really, too much,* or *overly.* Examples are:

napakaganda = *very* beautiful
napakatalino = *very* smart
ubod ng payat = *very* thin
saksakan ng bait = *very* kind
talagang masipag = *really* hardworking
sobrang init = *too* hot
masyadong emosyonal = *too* emotional

Just like the moderate degree, a partial/full reduplication may also occur with some adjectives to express its strong intensity. So, how will you know if the reduplicated adjective means moderate or intense? Look at the examples below:

mahirap *(difficult)* → **mahirap-hirap** *(a little difficult)* → **ang hirap-hirap** *(super difficult)*
maalat *(salty)* → **maalat-alat** *(a little salty)* → **ang alat-alat** *(super salty)*
mabilis *(quick)* → **mabilis-bilis** → *(a little quick)* → **ang bilis-bilis** *(super quick)*
madilim *(dark)* → **madilim-dilim** → *(a little dark)* → **ang dilim-dilim** *(super dark)*

In this case, it is important to know the root word of the adjective. From the previous chapter, you have learned that the basic forms of Tagalog adjectives are created by adding **ma** + noun, as in **maganda** (**ma** + *beauty* = *beautiful*). Looking at the examples above, if the **ma-** form of the adjective is reduplicated, this means moderate degree or *a little*. If only the root word is reduplicated and is preceded by **ang**, then the meaning changes to a strong intensity.

Examples:

Malakas ang radyo. = The radio is <u>loud</u>.
Malakas-lakas ang radyo. = The radio is <u>somewhat loud</u>.
Ang lakas-lakas ng radyo. = The radio is <u>too loud</u>.

Madali lang ang pagsusulit. = The quiz is just <u>easy</u>.
Madali-dali lang ang pagsusulit. = The quiz is a <u>little easy</u>.
Ang dali-dali ng pagsusulit. = The quiz is <u>very easy</u>.

 **EXERCISE #1**

Isalin ang mga sumusunod na parirala.
Translate the following phrases.

1. medyo sensitibo = _____

2. mapula-pula = _____

3. ubod ng tangkad = _____

4. talagang masayahin = _____

5. ang taba-taba = _____

6. madulas-dulas = _____

7. sobrang gwapo = _____

8. ang dilaw-dilaw = _____

9. saksakan nang sungit = _____

10. masigla-sigla = _____

COMMON NOUN AFFIXES

Just like in English, the addition of various affixes can change the entire meaning of Tagalog words. Let's see how they change the meanings of common nouns in Tagalog.

PLACE

When you add the suffix **-an/-han** to some Tagalog nouns, it becomes the place where that noun is present in large quantities.

Examples:

ROOT	MEANING	ROOT + AFFIX	NEW MEANING
aklat	book	aklat<u>an</u>	library
palay	rice grain	palay<u>an</u>	rice field
basura	garbage	basura<u>han</u>	garbage can
gulay	vegetable	gulay<u>an</u>	[1]vegetable field [2]vegetable store

TOOL

When attached to some nouns that can be measured (e.g., weight and time), the suffix **-an/-han** can also mean a tool used to measure the root word.

Examples:

ROOT	MEANING	ROOT + AFFIX	NEW MEANING
timbang	weight	timbang<u>an</u>	weighing scale
oras	time	oras<u>an</u>	clock
sukat	measurement	sukat<u>an</u>	[1]measuring tool [2]measuring standards

ABSTRACT

When the prefix **ka-** and the suffix **-an/-han** are added to Tagalog abstract nouns, their sense or meaning is slightly altered. The root word is treated as the basic meaning while the affixed word means *"the essence or quality of"*. Both words can still be used interchangeably.

ROOT	MEANING	ROOT + AFFIX	NEW MEANING
yaman	*wealth (both material and immaterial)*	kayamanan	*richness*
bata	*kid or baby*	kabataan	*youth; youthfulness*
ganda	*beauty*	kagandahan	*beauty*
talino	*intelligence*	katalinuhan	*intelligence*

GROUP OF THINGS/PEOPLE

Another use of affixes **ka-** and **-an/-han** is to connote a group or a range of nouns.

ROOT	MEANING	ROOT + AFFIX	NEW MEANING
babae	*woman*	kababaihan	*a group of women*
bundok	*mountain*	kabundukan	*mountain range*
dagat	*sea*	karagatan	*ocean*
pulo	*island*	kapuluan	*archipelago*

PERSONAL RELATIONSHIP

The prefix **mag-** is used to indicate two or more people in any type of relationship.

ROOT	MEANING	ROOT + AFFIX	NEW MEANING
asawa	*spouse*	mag-asawa	*husband & wife*
ina	*mother*	mag-ina	*mother and child*
kaibigan	*friend*	magkaibigan	*two friends*
pinsan	*cousin*	magpinsan	*two cousins*

COMPETITION

Another set of noun affixes is **pa- -an/-han** which means a contest or a competition. They are usually attached to abstract nouns and some measurable nouns.

ROOT	MEANING	ROOT + AFFIX	NEW MEANING
bigat	weight	pabigatan	weight contest
taas	height	pataasan	height contest
talino	intelligence	patalinuhan	intellect contest
ganda	beauty	pagandahan	beauty contest

OBJECT USED FOR SOMETHING

When the prefix **pang/pam-** is attached to a noun, its meaning becomes "an object that is used for a certain place or thing" (e.g., *slippers for the house, tools for the kitchen, etc.*) or "an object meant for a certain person" (e.g., *clothes for pregnant women, shoes for kids, etc.*).

ROOT	MEANING	ROOT + AFFIX	NEW MEANING
kusina	kitchen	pangkusina	an object specifically used for the kitchen
bahay	house	pangbahay/pambahay	an object specifically used for the house
eskwela	school	pang-eskwela	an object specifically used for school
nanay	mother	pangnanay	an object meant for moms

SEASON

The prefix **tag-** means a season or a period.

ROOT	MEANING	ROOT + AFFIX	NEW MEANING
ulan	rain	tag-ulan	rainy season
init	heat	tag-init	summer season
gutom	hunger	taggutom	a period when you don't have enough money to even afford food
lamig	coldness	taglamig	cold season

HOMETOWN/PLACE OF WORK

As mentioned in Section 1, the prefix **taga-** connotes that someone is from a certain place.

ROOT	MEANING	ROOT + AFFIX	NEW MEANING
probinsya	province	**taga**probinsya	someone from the province
Espanya	Spain	**taga**-Espanya	someone from Spain
gobyerno	government	**taga**gobyerno	someone from the government
Maynila	Manila	**taga**-Maynila	someone from Manila

IMITATION/PROXY

When the suffix **-an/-han** is preceded by a reduplication of the word, it means that it is fake or a replacement for the original one.

ROOT	MEANING	ROOT + AFFIX	NEW MEANING
nanay	mother	nanay-nanay<u>an</u>	foster or surrogate mother
bahay	house	bahay-bahay<u>an</u>	playhouse
amo	boss	amu-amu<u>han</u>	a person acting like the boss
baril	gun	baril-baril<u>an</u>	toy gun

MATE

When it pertains to someone you work with or are simply associated with, you add the prefix **ka-** to the noun.

ROOT	MEANING	ROOT + AFFIX	NEW MEANING
opisina	office	<u>ka</u>-opisina	officemate
klase	class	<u>ka</u>klase	classmate
grupo	group	<u>ka</u>grupo	groupmate
baro	clothes	<u>ka</u>baro	abstract: someone from the same social status, profession, race, etc.

Now let's try to use some of these nouns in a sentence.

Sumulat ang mga <u>kababaihan</u> kay Rizal. = *The <u>women</u> wrote to Rizal.*
Damit <u>pangbahay</u> lang ang suot ko. = *I'm just wearing <u>home clothes</u>.*
Ang <u>kabataan</u> ang pag-asa ng bayan. = *Our <u>youth</u> are the hope of the nation.*
<u>Tag-init</u> na sa Marso. = *It's <u>summer</u> already in March.*
Naglalaro ang bata ng <u>baril-barilan.</u> = *The kid is playing with a <u>toy gun</u>.*
<u>Mag-asawa</u> kami ni Richard. = *Richard and I are a <u>married couple</u>.*
Si Sheila ay <u>tagamunisipyo</u>. = *Sheila <u>works in the municipal hall</u>.*
Ang yaman ay hindi <u>sukatan</u> ng tagumpay. = *Wealth is not a <u>metric</u> for success.*
Magkikita kami ng <u>kaklase</u> ko mamaya. = *My <u>classmate</u> and I will meet later.*

EXERCISE #2

Piliin ang tamang lapi ayon sa kahulugan ng salita.
Choose the correct affix based on the meaning of the word.

1. _____-Bulacan *(someone from Bulacan)*

    a. pang-   b. -an   c. taga-

2. _____-laro *(someone you play with)*

    a. -han   b. ka-   c. tag-

3. _____-babae *(something specifically for women)*

    a. pang-   b. ka- -an   c. ka-

4. _____-lagas *(autumn season)*

    a. -an   b. tag-   c. taga-

5. kotse-kotse _____ *(toy car)*

    a. -han   b. pang-   c. -ka

6. _____ laya _____ *(freedom)*

    a. ka- -an   b. ka- -ang   c. ka- -pan

7. _____-opisina *(someone who works in the office)*

    a. taga-   b. pang-   c. ka-

8. _____-opisina *(something you use in the office)*

    a. taga-   b. pang-   c. ka-

9. _____-opisina *(officemate)*

    a. taga-   b. pang-   c. ka-

10. tatay-tatay _____ *(foster/surrogate father)*

    a. -an   b. tag-   c. ka- -an

DEMONSTRATIVE PRONOUNS

In the previous sections, you were introduced to **ito**, **iyon** and **iyan**, which may all refer to the pronoun *it*. Now we're digging a little deeper into the various demonstrative pronouns you can use in Tagalog. Unlike English where it's mainly *this* or *that*, Tagalog demonstrative pronouns vary in cases (direct object vs. indirect object, existential, etc.).

ITO, IYAN, IYON

If the pronoun is the subject of the sentence or the receiver of the action, you can use **ito**, **iyan**, and **iyon**.

ito	it/this (close to the speaker)
iyan	that (a little far from the speaker, nearer to the addressee)
iyon	that (far from both the speaker and addressee)

Examples:
Gusto ko ito. = *I like it.*
Kinuha ko itong panyo. = *I took this handkerchief.*
Iyan ba ang kotse mo? = *Is that your car?*
Paki-abot nga iyang papel sa harap mo. = *Please pass me that paper in front of you.*
Sino ang lalaking iyon? = *Who is that man?*
Magkano iyong sumbrero sa likod? = *How much is that cap at the back?*

NITO, NIYAN, NIYON

These pronouns are mainly used if you are referring to the actor/agent of the verb but can also be an object of the verb. They can refer both to things and people, and are usually used in informal conversations.

nito	it/this; he/she (close to the speaker)
niyan	that; he/she (nearer/more related to the addressee)
niyon	that; he/she (far from both the speaker and addressee)

Examples:
Kinuha ni John ang pitaka. → **Kinuha nito ang pitaka.** = *He took the wallet.*
Ang pagluto nito ay hindi madali. = *Cooking this is not easy.*

Hindi alam ng kaibigan mo. → **Hindi alam niyan.** = <u>He/she</u> *(friend near addressee) doesn't know.*
Tatamaan ka ng bola. → **Tatamaan ka niyan.** = <u>That</u> *(ball near addressee) will hit you.*

For the pronoun **niyon**, most native speakers use its contracted form **non/nun**.

Niloloko ka ng asawa mo. → **Niloloko ka nun.** = <u>He/she</u> *(spouse in topic, not present) is cheating on you.*

Nangangarap ako ng buong pamilya. → **Nangangarap ako nun.** = *I am dreaming of that (an abstract topic, currently far from reality).*

DITO, DIYAN, DOON

Now we move on to location. **Dito**, **diyan**, and **doon** are locative markers that indicate the place where the action is directed.

dito	*here (close to the speaker)*
diyan	*there (a little far from the speaker, nearer to the addressee)*
doon	*there (far from both the speaker and addressee)*

Examples:
Pumunta ka <u>dito</u>. = *Come <u>here</u>.*
<u>Dito</u> sila nagsimula. = *They started <u>here</u>.*

Lumiko ka <u>diyan</u>. = *Take a turn <u>there</u>.*
<u>Diyan</u> ako mauupo sa tabi mo. = *I will take a seat <u>there</u> beside you.*

Pupunta ako <u>doon</u> sa Amerika. = *I will go <u>there</u>, to America.*
<u>Doon</u> ako magpaPasko. = *I will spend Christmas <u>there</u>.*

NANDITO, NANDIYAN, NANDOON

Although these markers also mean *here* and *there*, they specifically refer to the location where someone/something exists.

nandito	*here (close to the speaker)*
nandiyan	*there (a little far from the speaker, nearer to the addressee)*
nandoon	*there (far from both the speaker and addressee)*

Examples:
Nandito ang tatay mo. = *Your father is <u>here</u>.*
Ang mga pulis ay <u>nandito</u> sa bahay. = *The police officers are <u>here</u> at the house.*

<u>**Nandiyan**</u> ba sa likod mo ang lapis ko? = *Is my pencil <u>there</u> at your back?*
<u>**Nandiyan**</u> na ang pagkain. = *The food is already <u>there</u>.*

<u>**Nandoon**</u> sa opisina si Grace. = *Grace is <u>there</u> at the office.*
<u>**Nandoon**</u> pa ba sa Maynila ang kotse? = *Is the car still <u>there</u> in Manila?*

ITO, IYAN, IYON

The last set of markers is used to express *here* and *there* in terms of showing/pointing/handing something to someone.

ito	*this/here (close to the speaker)*
iyan	*that/there (a little far from the speaker, nearer to the addressee)*
iyon	*that/there (far from both the speaker and addressee)*

Examples:
<u>**Ito**</u> na ang bayad ko. = <u>*Here*</u> *is my payment.*
<u>**Itong**</u> susi na lang kunin mo. = *Just get <u>these</u> keys right here.*
<u>**Iyan**</u> na siya! = <u>*There*</u> *he/she is!*
<u>**Iyang**</u> sapatos sa tabi mo ang kailangan ko. = <u>*Those*</u> *shoes beside you are what I need.*
<u>**Iyon**</u> ang bulalakaw sa malayo. = *The falling star is far <u>over there</u>.*
<u>**Iyong**</u> damit na nakasabit ba ang gusto mo? = *Do you like <u>that</u> hung shirt over there?*

ENCLITIC PARTICLES

The last grammar lesson for this section is the enclitic particle. An enclitic particle is a word that is mainly optional to the sentence but still conveys important information (e.g., *just* or *so*). Enclitic particles are essential in Tagalog as they usually determine the tone of the speech. They are mostly found near the beginning of the sentence, but never as the first word. Most of these particles do not have an English equivalent, so we will discuss the context behind their usage.

NA

The enclitic **na** means *now*, *already* or that something is final/already decided.

Examples:
Dumating na ang sweldo ko. = My salary is <u>already</u> credited.
Bukas na ako maghuhugas ng pinggan. = I will wash the dishes tomorrow. (With the use of **na**, it means the decision is final.)

PA

This means *still* or *yet*.

Examples:
Bukas pa ako maghuhugas ng pinggan. = I will wash the dishes tomorrow. (With the use of **pa**, you're emphasizing that you're not going to do it just yet.)
Nasa tren <u>pa</u> siya. = She is <u>still</u> on the train.

DAW

This is used by the speaker when quoting another person's statement, except the addressee's.

Examples:
Ayaw pa <u>daw</u> kumain ni Mama. = Mama said she does not want to eat yet.
Wala <u>daw</u> pasok bukas. = The announcement said there is no class tomorrow.

YATA

This word means the speaker is expressing his/her uncertainty about a statement or situation.

Examples:
Nalulunod <u>yata</u> 'yung bata! = I think that kid is drowning!
Hindi ko <u>yata</u> napanood ito. = I'm not sure if I have watched this.

NAMAN

This enclitic particle refers to the speaker's attempt to soften the statement or to emphasize something.

Examples:
Hindi <u>naman</u> ako galit. = I did not say I was angry.
Hindi ka <u>naman</u> nakikinig. = I can see that you're not even listening.

SANA

This means a statement is said with a tinge of hope or wishful thinking. It can also be used to express regret.

Examples:
Dalawin niya <u>sana</u> ako bukas. = *I hope he/she will visit me tomorrow.*
Muntik na <u>sana</u> ako manalo! = *I was so close to winning!*

PALA

You use **pala** when there is a sudden realization or when you just remembered something.

Examples:
Wala <u>pala</u> akong dalang pera! = *Oh, I have no money with me!*
Hindi <u>pala</u> niya ako minahal. = *Now I know he/she did not really love me.*

MUNA

This means *for now*.

Examples:
Hindi <u>muna</u> ako sasama. = *For now, I'm not coming with you.*
Pwede bang tumahimik ka <u>muna</u>? = *Can you just keep quiet for a bit?*

NGA

This word can both soften a statement and reinforce a certain point.

Examples:
Ako <u>nga</u> ang magbabayad. = *I told you, I'll be the one to pay.*
Kunin mo <u>nga</u> ang suklay. = *Get the comb. (With the use of **nga**, you're softening the tone, but it would still not equate to saying please.)*

 **EXERCISE #3**

Piliin ang salitang pinakaangkop sa pangungusap.
Choose the word that best fits the sentence.

```
A. muna        F. ito
B. nandito     G. doon
C. nga         H. na
D. daw         I. pala
E. sana        J. nandiyan
```

1. _____ na ang pagkain mo.
Here's your food.

2. Sumama ka _____ sabi ni Tom.
Tom said you should join us.

3. Pagod _____ ako.
I am already tired.

4. _____ sa kwarto ko ang gamit mo.
Your things are here in my room.

5. Pangalan mo _____ ang tinatawag!
It's your name being called! (emphasis)

6. Titira ako _____ sa Tsina.
I am going to live there in China.

7. _____ bumagal ang oras.
I hope time slows down.

8. Magpapahinga _____ kaming lahat.
We will all take a rest for now.

9. Hindi ko namalayang alas-dose na _____!
   I didn't realize it was already 12!

10. _____ sa bulsa mo ang tiket.
    The ticket is there in your pocket.

🎧 LISTENING #1

Makinig at bilugan ang titik ng tamang sagot.
Listen to the recording and answer the questions by encircling the letter of the correct answer.

1. The television show's description.
   a. masyadong emosyonal   **b.** napakatalino   **c.** ubod ng payat

2. The physical trait of the woman being shown on television.
   a. masyadong emosyonal   **b.** napakatalino   **c.** ubod ng payat

3. The description of the woman's child.
   a. masyadong emosyonal   **b.** napakatalino   **c.** ubod ng payat

4. The environment where the woman is.
   a. madilim-dilim   **b.** malungkot   **c.** matanda

5. The description of the background music.
   a. madilim-dilim   **b.** malungkot   **c.** matanda

B. VOCABULARY

As previously mentioned, the goal of this section is to improve your vocabulary of terms relating to people and places outside of your home. It aims to answer questions such as: *How is your neighborhood* or *What kind of people do you work with?*

NEIGHBORHOOD

The Filipino culture is big on the concept of **kapwa-tao** which means caring for your neighbor/others. Communities are so tight-knit that sharing food with your neighbors on a daily basis is a common sight! Here are some terms you can use to describe your house and neighborhood:

kapitbahay – *neighbor*
kapitbahayan – *neighborhood*
kabayan – *someone from the same hometown*
barangay – *smallest district in the Philippines*
kapitan/kapitana – *barangay captain*
kagawad – *barangay council member*
tanod – *barangay custodian/guard*
sabdibisyon – *subdivision*
paupahan – *apartment*
lote – *lot*
kalye – *street*
kanto – *corner*
tirahan – *address*
bahay – *house*

kusina – *kitchen*
silid/kwarto – *room*
sala – *living room*
bubong – *roof*
bintana – *window*
pader – *wall*
geyt – *gate*
pinto – *door*
palengke – *market*
simbahan – *church*
istasyon ng pulis – *police station*
kainan – *restaurant*
eskwelahan/paaralan - *school*
parke – *park*

Useful adjectives to describe your neighbor and neighborhood:

malawak – *wide*
malayo – *far*
malapit – *near*
masikip/maraming tao – *crowded*
mayaman – *rich*
mahirap – *poor*
makabago – *modern*
makaluma – *old-fashioned*

tahimik – *quiet*
maingay – *loud/noisy*
matulungin – *helpful*
palangiti – *always smiling*
makwento – *chatty*
palakaibigan – *friendly*
madamot – *selfish*
walang pakialam – *indifferent*

Here are some sample sentences you can use to talk about your neighborhood:

Malaki ang lote ng kapitbahay ko. = *My neighbor's lot is wide.*
Saan ang tirahan mo? = *What is your address?*
Sa Maynila ako nakatira. = *I live in Manila.*
Malayo ang palengke mula sa bahay ko. = *The market is far from my house.*
Pipinturahan niya ang bubong niya. = *He/She is going to paint his/her roof.*
Nagpatawag ang kapitan ng pulong. = *The captain called for a meeting.*
Mababait ang aking mga kapitbahay. = *My neighbors are kind.*
Tahimik ang aming kapitbahayan. = *Our neighborhood is quiet.*
Maliit lang ang kwarto ko sa bahay. = *My room at home is just small.*
Sarado ang simbahan tuwing Lunes. = *The church is closed on Mondays.*
Ang barangay namin ay malinis. = *Our district is clean.*
Makabago ang disenyo ng kaniyang bahay. = *His/Her house has a modern design.*

WORKPLACE

Another integral part of a Filipino's daily life is their place of work. Here are some vocabulary words to help you talk about your workplace:

opisina – *office*
ka-opisina – *officemate*
tagapamahala – *manager/overseer*
empleyado – *employee*
kasamahan – *companion (usually used in the context of workplace)*
amo – *boss*
kliyente – *client*
kasosyo sa negosyo – *business partner*
kostumer – *customer*
tindero/tindera – *salesman/saleslady*
weyter – *waiter*
gwardiya – *guard*
tagabangko – *bank employee*
drayber – *driver*
dentista – *dentist*
arkitekto – *architect*

inhinyero – *engineer*
musikero – *musician*
kasambahay – *maid*
aplikante – *applicant*
sweldo – *salary*
kumpanya – *company*
korporasyon – *corporation*
pabrika – *factory*
trabaho – *job*
ekonomiya – *economy*
papasok sa trabaho – *going to work*
uuwi galing sa trabaho – *coming home from work*

Useful adjectives to describe your workplace and the people you work with:

madali – *easy*
mahirap – *difficult*
mababang sweldo – *low salary*
mataas na sweldo – *high salary*
may trabaho – *employed*
walang trabaho – *unemployed*
magaan na trabaho – *light work*
mabigat na trabaho – *heavy work*
mahigpit – *strict*

nakakapagod – *tiring/demanding*
nakakabagot – *boring*
organisado – *organized*
may tiwala sa sarili – *self-confident*
ganado – *motivated/driven*
masipag – *hardworking*
panktwal/laging maaga – *always punctual*
laging huli – *always late*
mapanganib – *dangerous*

Here are some sample sentences you can use to talk about your work:

Talagang mahigpit ang aking amo. = *My boss is really strict.*
Nagtatrabaho ako sa bangko. = *I work at a bank.*
Si Jem ay walang trabaho. = *Jem is unemployed.*
Mabait ang aking kasamahan. = *My workmate is kind.*
Madali lang ang gawain. = *The task is easy.*
Ganado ako magtrabaho dahil sa pamilya ko. = *I am driven to work because of my family.*
Mababa ang sweldo ko bilang weyter. = *My salary is low as a waiter.*
Si Ginoong Lim ay kostumer ko. = *Mr. Lim is my customer.*
Laging huli si Jan sa trabaho. = *Jan is always late for work.*
Mapanganib ang kaniyang trabaho. = *His/her work is dangerous.*

SOCIETY

The last part is talking about your community and the people in society. Here are some vocabulary words to help you talk about your community:

lipunan – *society*
bayan/nasyon – *nation*
komunidad – *community*
pamahalaan/gobyerno – *government*
republika – *republic*
demokrasya – *democracy*
diktadurya – *dictatorship*
pederalismo – *federalism*
komunismo – *communism*

politiko – *politician*
presidente/pangulo – *president*
bise presidente/pangalawang pangulo – *vice president*
gabinete – *cabinet members*
senado – *senate*
senador – *senator*
alkalde – *mayor*
bise alkalde – *vice mayor*

gobernador – *governor*
bise gobernador – *vice governor*
militar – *military*
sundalo – *soldier*
pari – *priest*

madre – *nun*
pastor – *pastor*
tradisyon – *tradition*
kultura – *culture*
batas – *law*

Useful adjectives to describe your community and the people in it:

magaling – *excellent*
mapagkakatiwalaan – *trustworthy*
matapang – *brave*
matagumpay – *successful*
simple/payak – *simple*
maayos – *orderly*
magulo – *disorderly*
edukado – *educated*

sistemisado – *systematized*
masama – *evil*
maswerte – *fortunate*
malas – *unfortunate*
populado – *populated*
urbanisado – *urbanized*
rural – *rural*
sibilisado – *civilized*

Here are some sample sentences you can use to talk about your community:

Magulo ang komunidad namin. (Our community is disorderly.)
Magaling ba ang mga lider ng bansa? (Are the leaders of the country excellent?)
Dapat kilalaning mabuti ang mga politiko. (We should scrutinize politicians.)
Maraming mahihigpit na batas sa lugar namin. (There are a lot of strict rules in our place.)
Simple lang ang pamumuhay ko. (My way of living is just simple.)
Mapagkakatiwalaan ang pari sa parokya namin. (The priest in our church is trustworthy.)
Dapat pagyamanin ang mga tradisyon natin. (We should enrich our traditions.)
Ang Maynila ay isang urbanisadong syudad. (Manila is an urbanized city.)
Matatapang ang mga sundalong Pilipino. (The Filipino soldiers are brave.)

EXERCISE #4

A. Tukuyin ang mga miyembro ng lipunan ayon sa larawan.
Identify the member of society based on the illustration.

1.
_____

5.
_____

2.
_____

6.
_____

3.
_____

7.
_____

4.
_____

8.
_____

B. Piliin ang angkop na salita sa pangungusap.
Choose the correct word for the sentence.

1. Gusto kong maging _____. *(I want to become a _____.)*
   a. gobyerno   b. sundalo   c. lipunan

2. Ang kapitbahay ko ay _____. *(My neighbor is _____.)*
   a. maulan   b. madali   c. matulungin

3. Ang mga Pilipinong magsasaka ay _____. *(Filipino farmers are _____.)*
   a. masisipag   b. nakakabagot   c. masisikip

4. Magkano ang _____ bilang isang guro? *(How much is the _____ for a teacher?)*
   a. palengke   b. sweldo   c. gabinete

5. Ang Pilipinas ay isang _____ bansa. *(The Philippines is a _____ country.)*
   a. militar   b. mabigat   c. populado

6. Demokratiko ang uri ng _____ sa bansa. *(The type of _____ in the country is democratic.)*
   a. gobyerno   b. komunidad   c. barangay

7. Magluluto ako sa _____. *(I will cook in the _____.)*
   a. bubong   b. kusina   c. kwarto

8. Mangungumpisal ako sa _____ bukas. *(I will confess to a _____ tomorrow.)*
   a. dentista   b. pari   c. drayber

9. Ang _____ ang papalit sa presidente. *(The _____ will replace the president.)*
   a. alkalde   b. senador   c. bise presidente

10. Nagtatrabaho ako sa _____ ng langis. *(I work at an oil _____).*
    a. kumpanya   b. pamahalaan   c. senado

LISTENING #2

Makinig at bilugan ang titik ng tamang sagot.
Listen to the recording and answer the questions by encircling the letter of the correct answer.

1. Which is near the speaker's house?

    a. market   b. school

2. Who is the barangay captain in Barangay Poblacion?

    a. Teddy Arevallo   b. Mark Cruz

3. Who is the sixteenth vice president of the Philippines?

    a. Rodrigo Duterte   b. Leni Robredo

4. Each Philippine town has one _____

    a. senator   b. mayor

5. Where do we find big corporations?

    a. Laguna   b. Makati

SECTION 5

TARA, MAGLIBOT TAYO
COME ON, LET'S MOVE AROUND

This section focuses on one thing—*action*. How do you express a movement or an incident in Tagalog? Grammar teaches you everything you need to know about conjugating verbs. As you might have expected, conjugating Tagalog verbs can be tricky, what with all the affixes and spelling changes. In addition, unlike English, Tagalog verbs don't change based on just tenses. Their forms differ based on an action's focus and intention. They're all about aspects.

Additionally, you will learn how to modify your verbs by knowing which adverb to add to them. This section will enrich your vocabulary with verbs that you can use in various settings—at school, at home, or even during your travel!

A. GRAMMAR

Verb conjugation is the process of changing a verb's form to express a difference in its tense, number, or focus. An excellent example in English is the verb *be*. It becomes *am* when partnered with *I*, *is* when the subject is singular, and *are* when the subject is plural. Changing its tenses, it becomes *was*, *is*, and *will be*. Simple, isn't it? Well, not exactly. Tagalog takes more things into consideration than just tenses. Tagalog verbs change depending on whether your action is intentional or not, who did it, and how you did it, among many others. Let's begin with the affixes.

FIVE BASIC VERB AFFIXES

MAG-

The most common basic verb affix of them all is **mag-** at the beginning of a verb. These verbs are inflected by the base affix **mag-** which indicates if the action is completed, progressive, or contemplative. These are actor-focused verbs (doer of the action), which means they cannot be used in a passive voice, as in *The wallet was stolen* or *The task is completed*.

So, how do you conjugate these verbs?

Past → **mag-** changes to **nag-** + *root verb*

Present → **mag-** changes to **nag-** + *reduplication of the first syllable + root verb*

Future → **mag-** + *reduplication of the first syllable + root verb*

ROOT VERB	PAST	PRESENT	FUTURE
lakad – to walk	naglakad	naglalakad	maglalakad
laro – to play	naglaro	naglalaro	maglalaro
bigay – to give	nagbigay	nagbibigay	magbibigay
ipon – to save	nag-ipon	nag-iipon	mag-iipon
aral – to study	nag-aral	nag-aaral	mag-aaral

Note from the last two examples that when this affix is added to a verb that starts with a vowel, a hyphen is added after the affix.

If you want to form an imperative, simply add **mag-** to the root verb as follows:

Huwag kang magsugal. = *Don't gamble. (Root verb: sugal)*
Huwag kang magtampo. = *Don't be upset. (Root verb: tampo)*
Huwag kang mag-alala. = *Don't worry. (Root verb: alala)*

Examples:
Si Alyssa ay nagluto kagabi. = *Alyssa cooked last night. (Root verb: luto)*
Magpapakasal ka na ba? = *Are you getting married? (Root verb: kasal)*
Naglaba ako kahapon. = *I did the laundry yesterday. (Root verb: laba)*
Nagsasayaw ang bata. = *The child is dancing. (Root verb: sayaw)*
Magtatampo si Anton kapag hindi ka sumama. = *Anton will get upset if you don't join us.*
 (Root verb: tampo)

MA-

Another type of Tagalog verb is those that begin with **ma-**. These verbs are similar to **mag-** verbs in terms of their conjugation. **Ma-** verbs are also actor-focused but can also be object-focused (receiver of the action).

Past → **ma-** changes to **na-** + *root verb*

Present → **ma-** changes to **na-** + *reduplication of the first syllable + root verb*

Future → **ma-** + *reduplication of the first syllable + root verb*

ROOT VERB	PAST	PRESENT	FUTURE
kinig – to listen	nakinig	nakikinig	makikinig
basa – to get wet	nabasa	nababasa	mababasa
sunog – to burn	nasunog	nasusunog	masusunog
bangga – to crash	nabangga	nababangga	mababangga
sira – to break	nasira	nasisira	masisira

To form the imperative, just add **ma-** to the root verb:

Maligo ka na. = *Take a shower* now. (Root verb: **ligo**)
Huwag kang **manood**. = *Don't watch*. (Root verb: **nood**)
Matulog ka na. = *Get some sleep* now. (Root verb: **tulog**)

Examples:
Malalaman ni Sheila ang katotohanan. = *Sheila will find out* the truth. (Root verb: **laman**)
Bulalakaw ba iyong **nakikita** ko? = *Is that a comet I am seeing?* (Root verb: **kita**)
Nabasag ang paso. = *The pot was broken*. (Root verb: **basag**)
Masosorpresa si inay sa regalo ko. = *Mom will be surprised* with my gift. (Root verb: **sorpresa**)
Ang guro ay **nagalit**. = *The teacher got angry*. (Root verb: **galit**)

-UM-

The infix **-um-** is another affix added to some Tagalog verbs to indicate its tense. These are actor-focused verbs. Its conjugation is different from the first two types of verbs as the affix is inserted inside the root verb.

Past → *first letter of the root verb + -um- + the rest of the word/letters*
Present → *first letter of the root verb + -um- + first vowel of the word + root verb*
Future → *reduplication of the first syllable + **root verb***

ROOT VERB	PAST	PRESENT	FUTURE
sigaw – to shout	sumigaw	sumisigaw	sisigaw
tawa – to laugh	tumawa	tumatawa	tatawa
kain – to eat	kumain	kumakain	kakain
upo – to sit	umupo	umuupo	uupo
ngiti – to smile	ngumiti	ngumingiti	ngingiti

Notice how in the fourth example, **um** is added at the beginning of the word. This happens when the root verb starts with a vowel. As for the word **ngiti** in the fifth example, **ng** is considered as one sound/entity so you should add the **um** after the **g** and not its first letter.

Forming an imperative with these verbs can be confusing as their imperatives are the same form as their past tense. The difference will depend on the context of your conversation and the sentence construction. If **ka** (you) is added after the verb, it is most likely a command:

<u>Tumayo</u> ka. = <u>Stand up</u>. (Root verb: **tayo**)
(can also mean: You stood up.)
<u>Tumigil</u> ka. = <u>Stop</u>. (Root verb: **tigil**)
(can also mean: You stopped.)
<u>Umalis</u> ka ng bahay ko. = <u>Get out</u> of my house. (Root verb: **alis**)
(can also mean: You got out of my house.)

Examples:
<u>Umiyak</u> si Claire kanina. = Claire <u>cried</u> a while ago. (Root verb: **iyak**)
Araw-araw <u>pumapasok</u> sa eskwela si George. = George <u>goes to school</u> every day. (Root verb: **pasok**)
<u>Uulan</u> mamaya. = It <u>will rain</u> later. (Root verb: **ulan**)
<u>Sasama</u> ka ba sa amin? = <u>Will</u> you <u>join</u> us later? (Root verb: **sama**)
Si tatay ang <u>bumili</u> ng sapatos ko. = Papa <u>bought</u> my shoes. (Root verb: **bili**)

-IN-

Another infix, **-in-** is inserted mostly in object-focused verbs. This means that the highlight of the action is not the doer but its receiver.

Past → *first letter of the root verb + **-in-** + the rest of the word/letters*
Present → *first letter of the root verb + **-in-** + first vowel of the word + root verb*
Future → *reduplication of the first syllable + root verb + **-in***

ROOT VERB	PAST	PRESENT	FUTURE
gupit – to cut	ginupit	ginugupit	gugupitin
patay – to turn off	pinatay	pinapatay	papatayin
hintay – to wait	hinintay	hinihintay	hihintayin
yakap – to hug	niyakap	niyayakap	yayakapin
sundo – to pick up	sinundo	sinusundo	susunduin

In the third example, **yakap**, **in** becomes **ni** when the root verb starts with letters **l**, **y**, and **r**. It is also placed at the beginning of the word. So, from the root verb **yakap**, we don't say **yinakap** to mean *hugged*. Instead, we say **niyakap**.

Lastly, the fourth example, **sundo**, shows us that when the last syllable of the root verb has a letter **o**, it changes to **u** when creating its future form. Example, the verb **ayos** means to fix; **inayos** means fixed, and **inaayos** means fixing. If you want to say you will fix something, you don't say **aayosin**. Instead, you change **o** to **u** as in **aayusin**. Forming the imperative for these verbs is just like forming their future tenses, without the reduplication of the first syllable:

<u>Mahalin</u> mo ako. = <u>Love me</u>. (Root verb: **mahal**)
Huwag mo akong <u>awayin</u>. = *Don't <u>fight</u> me*. (Root verb: **away**)
<u>Linisin</u> mo ang kotse. = <u>Clean</u> *the car*. (Root verb: **linis**)

Examples:
<u>Sinuri</u> ni Carmen ang mga papeles. = *Carmen <u>examined</u> the papers*. (Root verb: **suri**)
<u>Isipin</u> mong mabuti. = <u>Think</u> *about it carefully*. (Root verb: **isip**)
<u>Tatawagin</u> ng nars ang iyong pangalan. = *The nurse <u>will call</u> your name*. (Root verb: **tawag**)
<u>Inalok</u> ko siya ng pagkain. = *I <u>offered</u> him/her some food*. (Root verb: **alok**)
<u>Winalis</u> ko ang kalat. = *I <u>swept</u> the dirt*. (Root verb: **walis**)

i-

You can find a lot of similarities between the **i-** and **-in-** verbs. Aside from being both object-focused verbs, their conjugation patterns are also similar. The main difference lies in how you form their future tense, as seen below:

Past → **i-** + *first letter of the root verb* + **-in-** + *the rest of the word/letters*
Present → **i-** + *first letter of the root verb* + **-in-** + *first vowel of the word* + *root verb*
Future → **i-** + *reduplication of the first syllable* + *root verb*

ROOT VERB	PAST	PRESENT	FUTURE
bigay – *to give*	ibinigay	ibinibigay	ibibigay
sulat – *to write*	isinulat	isinusulat	isusulat
bunyag – *to reveal*	ibinunyag	ibinubunyag	ibubunyag
balik – *to return*	ibinalik	ibinabalik	ibabalik
tanggi – *to deny*	itinanggi	itinatanggi	itatanggi

To form the imperative, simply attach the prefix **i-** to the root verb:

Ihinto mo ang sasakyan. = _Stop the car._ (Root verb: **hinto**)
Huwag mong **ilabas** ang gamit mo. = _Don't take out your things._ (Root verb: **labas**)
Isabit mo ang orasan sa pader. = _Hang the clock on the wall._ (Root verb: **sabit**)

Examples:
Ibinato niya ang kaniyang sapatos. = _He/She threw his/her shoes._ (Root verb: **bato**)
Ibabawas ko ba ang bayad dito? = _Will I subtract the payment here?_ (Root verb: **bawas**)
Itinaas ko ang upuan. = _I raised the chair._ (Root verb: **taas**)
Isinasara na nila ang pintuan. = _They are closing the door._ (Root verb: **sara**)
Isasali kita sa aming grupo. = _I will include you in our group._ (Root verb: **sali**)

So, now that you are familiar with the 5 basic types of Tagalog verbs, you may be wondering: _"How will I know which affixes to use on each verb?"_ Unfortunately, there is no general rule to determine whether a verb is a **mag-** or an **i-** verb. It all boils down to how well you memorize each form and for what context they should be used in—nothing that a little practice can't solve.

For instance, the root verb **lakad** _(to walk)_ can be used with all five affixes, depending on the context of your conversation. Take a look at the difference in their meanings:

Naglakad si Sophia. = _Sophia walked._
Nalakad ni Sophia ang daan. = _Sophia was able to walk on the road._
Lumakad si Sophia. = _Sophia (intentionally) walked._
Nilakad ni Sophia ang daan. = _Sophia walked on the road._
Inilakad ni Sophia ang kaniyang aso. = _Sophia walked her dog._

Complicated? Don't worry. There's an in-depth discussion on the semantic implications of verb affixes in the following sections.

EXERCISE #1

A. Isulat ang wastong anyo ng pandiwa.
Write the correct form of the verb.

MAG-

ROOT VERB	PAST	PRESENT	FUTURE
alay – *to offer*	nag-alay	1.	mag-aalay
sabi – *to say*	2.	nagsasabi	3.
paalam – *to ask for permission*	4.	5.	magpapaalam

MA-

ROOT VERB	PAST	PRESENT	FUTURE
manhid – *to feel numb*	namanhid	6.	7.
lito – *to get confused*	8.	nalilito	malilito
buhat – *to carry*	9.	nabubuhat	10.

-UM-

ROOT VERB	PAST	PRESENT	FUTURE
alis – *to leave*	umalis	umaalis	11.
baba – *to go down*	bumaba	12.	bababa
palpak – *to fail*	13.	pumapalpak	14.

-IN-

ROOT VERB	PAST	PRESENT	FUTURE
pilit – *to insist*	pinilit	15.	16.
mithi – *to desire*	17.	minimithi	mimithiin
kain – *to eat*	kinain	18.	19.

I-

ROOT VERB	PAST	PRESENT	FUTURE
kabit – *to attach*	20.	ikinakabit	21.
sama – *to include*	22.	23.	isasama
sulat – *to write*	isinulat	24.	25.

B. Tukuyin ang ugat-pandiwa base sa mga larawan.
Identify the root verbs based on the illustrations.

1.

2.

3.

4.

5.

6.

7.

OTHER VERB AFFIXES

Now that you know the five primary verb affixes, it's time to move on to these more complex affixes. You may use these affixes in addition to a base verb (non-conjugated) or a verb that already has basic affixes (conjugated) to change its meaning and focus.

-HAN/-AN

When you add the suffix **-han** or **-an** to **mag-** or **-um** verbs, there are two possible semantic changes: 1) the action was performed by a group of people/things, or 2) the action is reciprocal.

Examples:

1) Collective Action

ROOT VERB	WITHOUT -HAN/-AN	WITH -HAN/-AN
alis – to leave	Umalis ang mga pulis. The police officers left.	Nag-alisan ang mga pulis. The police officers all left together.
kanta – to sing	Kakanta ba tayo? Are we going to sing?	Magkakantahan ba tayo? Are we going to sing together?

2) Reciprocal Action

ROOT VERB	WITHOUT -HAN/-AN	WITH -HAN/-AN
halik – to kiss	Humahalik ang bata sa santo. The child is kissing the saint's statue.	Naghahalikan sila. They are kissing each other.
biro – to joke/tease	Nagbiro si Jake. Jake told a joke.	Nagbiruan sina Jake at Paul. Jake and Paul teased each other.

Note that we add **-han** if the verb ends with a vowel and **-an** if it ends with a consonant. Moreover, if the last syllable has the letter **o**, it automatically changes to **u** before attaching the **-han/-an** suffix, as in **biro** – **biruan**.

Now, what happens if we add the suffix **-han/-an** to the remaining three verbs that begin with **ma-**, **-in-**, and **i-**? Two changes in meaning can occur: 1) the verb highlights the affected area/object/person of the action, or 2) the verb highlights the direction where the action is headed/coming from.

Examples:

1) Emphasizing the recipient/affected entity of the action

ROOT VERB	WITHOUT -HAN/-AN	WITH -HAN/-AN
sunog – to burn	Nasunog ang bahay ni Jennie. *Jennie's house was on fire.*	Nasunugan ng bahay si Jennie. *Jennie is a victim of a house fire.*
dilig – to water	Nagdilig si Josh ng mga halaman. *Josh watered the plants.* *(The focus here is the doer of the action, Josh.)*	Diniligan ni Josh ang mga halaman. *Josh watered the plants.* *(The focus here becomes the receiver of the action, the plants.)*

2) Emphasizing the direction of the action

ROOT VERB	WITHOUT -HAN/-AN	WITH -HAN/-AN
punta – to go	Napunta ako sa palengke. *I went to the market* *(The focus here is the doer of the action, "ako" or the speaker.)*	Napuntahan ko ang palengke. *I was able to go to the market.* *(The focus here becomes the direction or place the action was taken, the market.)*
takbo – to run	Tinakbo ko ang kalsada. *I ran on the road.*	Tinakbuhan ko ang sasakyan. *I ran away from the car.*

IPANG-

Another affix that you can add to verbs is ipang-. It highlights the tool that the actor used to complete the action. This affix follows the conjugation pattern of -i- verbs for its past, present, and future forms.

Examples:

ROOT VERB	WITHOUT IPANG-	WITH IPANG-
lakad – *to walk*	<u>Lalakad</u> ako sa dalampasigan. *I <u>will walk</u> on the shore.*	<u>Ipanlalakad</u> ko ang tsinelas ko sa dalampasigan. *I will use <u>my slippers to walk on</u> the shore.*
bayad – *to pay*	<u>Nagbayad</u> ako ng utang ko. *I <u>paid</u> my debt.*	<u>Ipinambayad</u> ko ng utang ang aking ipon. *I used <u>my savings to pay for</u> my debt.*
alis – *to remove*	<u>Inaalis</u> ko ang mantsa. *I <u>am removing</u> the stain.*	<u>Ipinang-aalis</u> ko ng mantsa ang sabon. *I am using <u>the soap to remove</u> the stain.*

Note that when you use the affix **ipang-**, you should follow these various phonetic rules:

When the root verb starts with **l** and **d**, **ipang-** becomes **ipan** + *root verb*.
    Ex. **laban** (*to fight*) = <u>**ipanlaban**</u> (*to fight using x*)
    dakma (*to grab*) = <u>**ipandakma**</u> (*to grab using x*)

When the root verb starts with **b** and **p**, **ipang-** becomes **ipam** + *root verb*.
    Ex. **bato** (*to throw*) = <u>**ipambato**</u> (*to throw using x*)
    pautang (*to lend money*) = <u>**ipampautang**</u> (*to lend money using x*)

When the root verb starts with **s** and **t**, **ipang-** becomes **ipan**, then the first letter of the root verb is dropped.
    Ex. **sakit** (*to hurt*) = <u>**ipanakit**</u> (*to hurt using x*)
    takot (*to scare*) = <u>**ipanakot**</u> (*to scare using x*)

When the root verb starts with **k**, **ipang-** is attached after the first letter of the root verb is dropped.
    Ex. **kalap** (*to search/collect*) = <u>**ipangalap**</u> (*to search/collect using x*)
    kulay (*to color*) = <u>**ipangulay**</u> (*to color using x*)

When the root verb starts with a vowel, **ipang-** is attached with a hyphen.
    Ex. **amoy** (*to smell*) = <u>**ipang-amoy**</u> (*to smell using x*)
    ukit (*to carve*) = <u>**ipang-ukit**</u> (*to carve using x*)

IKA-

The prefix **ika-** is added to verbs to signify the reason or the trigger of the action. Just like **ipang-**, it follows the conjugation pattern of **-in-** verbs to form its past, present, and future.

Examples:

ROOT VERB	WITHOUT IKA-	WITH IKA-
bahala – to worry	Nabahala ako. *I got worried.*	Ikinabahala ko ang iyong pag-alis. *Your departure got me worried.*
galit – to get angry	Magagalit si Inay. *Mom will get angry.*	Ikagagalit ni Inay ang pagiging tamad mo. *Your laziness will get Mom angry.*
yaman – to get rich	Yumayaman na ako paunti-unti. *I am slowly getting rich.*	Ikinayayaman ko ang aking negosyo. *My business is making me rich.*

KAKA-

The last verb affix to learn is **kaka-** which indicates that the action was just recently completed. **Kaka-** is attached directly to the root verb. It is usually followed by the word *lang* which translates to just.

ROOT VERB	PAST	PRESENT	FUTURE	RECENTLY COMPLETED
bihis – to get dressed	nagbihis	nagbibihis	magbibihis	kakabihis (lang) – *just got dressed*
gising – to wake up	gumising	gumigising	gigising	kakagising (lang) – *just woke up*
inom – to drink	uminom	umiinom	iinom	kakainom (lang) – *just drank*

Examples:

Kakakain ko lang ng tinapay. = *I just ate* a piece of bread. (Root verb: **kain**)
Kakasuot lang niya ng sombrero. = *He/She just wore* the hat. (Root verb: **suot**)
Kakalagay ko lang ng mantika. = *I just put* the oil. (Root verb: **lagay**)

Some natives use **ka-** + *reduplication of the first syllable + root verb*, as in **kagigising** instead of **kakagising**. Both forms can be used.

NOTES ON USING VERB AFFIXES

Conjugating Tagalog verbs can be daunting for complete beginners. That's why you should take your time studying them carefully. What does this mean?

- First, focus on the five basic types of verb affixes. Remember that **mag-**, **ma-** and **-um-** verbs are used when the subject is the actor/doer of the action, while **-in-** and **i-** verbs are used when the subject is the object of the action. Memorize the formula for conjugating each verb type for past, present, and future tenses. It is essential to be careful with the phonetic changes when attaching these affixes to the root verb.

- Once you are confident of your conjugation skills with the five basic affixes, it's time to move on to the next batch of affixes. With these additional affixes, it is essential to focus on knowing what each affix can do to the verb's meaning. What does it highlight—the trigger for the action? The instrument used? The beneficiary? You must be aware of the context. As discussed earlier, the conjugation pattern for the tenses is similar to that of the **in-** and **i-** verbs:

bayad *(to pay)* **i-**	*(to pay using x)* **ipang-**
ib<u>in</u>ayad	ip<u>in</u>ambayad
ib<u>in</u>abayad	ip<u>in</u>ambabayad
ib<u>a</u>bayad	ipamb<u>a</u>bayad

- Lastly, remember that while Tagalog verbs are generally not exclusive to just one type/affix, some verbs cannot take certain affixes. There are verbs that may take *all* affixes, while some might be used only with specific affixes. For instance, the verb *lakad (to walk)* can both change to **naglakad** *(walked)* and **lumakad** *(walked)*. **Kain** *(to eat)* on the other hand, takes the affix **-um-** as in **kumain** *(ate)* but never **nag-**. We cannot say **nagkain**. It takes consistent practice to familiarize yourself with contexts that allow a certain verb to use a certain affix. Luckily, this workbook is built to guide you through both the basics and complexities of Tagalog verbs.

EXERCISE #2

Piliin ang tamang anyo ng pandiwa.
Choose the correct form of the verb.

_____ 1. She <u>paid</u> the bill.
    a. nagbayad   b. pinambayad   c. kakabayad

_____ 2. I <u>just woke up</u>.
    a. kakagising   b. ginising   c. nanggising

_____ 3. The news <u>saddened</u> her.
    a. lungkot   b. ikinalungkot   c. nalulungkot

_____ 4. I <u>tried to kiss</u> someone.
    a. manghalik   b. hahalikan   c. hahalik

_____ 5. <u>Eat</u> now.
    a. kakain   b. ipangangain   c. kumain

_____ 6. Jessica <u>will walk</u>.
    a. maglalakad   b. naglalakad   c. nanlakad

_____ 7. I <u>will use</u> my card <u>to pay</u>.
    a. ipambabayad   b. nagbayad   c. magbabayad

_____ 8. The baby <u>accidentally wet</u> the floor.
    a. binasa   b. nabasa   c. basa

_____ 9. I <u>went to the market</u>.
    a. pupunta   b. nagpunta   c. magpupunta

_____ 10. <u>Will</u> you <u>join</u> the group for dinner?
    a. sasama   b. sumama   c. kakasama

VERB AFFIXES + LOANWORDS

Another fascinating thing about Tagalog verb conjugation is that Tagalog affixes can be integrated with English loanwords. Since English is the language of business and academics in the Philippines, owing to its status as an official language, loanwords follow the same grammatical rules. Thus, they are treated like native words. Many Filipinos code-switch between Tagalog and English (colloquially known as *Taglish*) in their everyday conversations. Here are some examples of English verbs with Tagalog affixes:

MAG-

ENGLISH VERB	PAST	PRESENT	FUTURE	IMPERATIVE
text	**nag**-text	**nag**te-text	**mag**te-text	**mag**-text
try	**nag**-try	**nag**ta-try	**mag**ta-try	**mag**-try

Nag-text ba si John sa iyo? = *Did John text you?*
Mag-try ka ng ibang damit. = *Try another dress.*

MA-

ENGLISH VERB	PAST	PRESENT	FUTURE	IMPERATIVE
break	**na**-break	**na**be-break	**ma**be-break	**i**-break
push	**na**-push	**na**pu-push	**ma**pu-push	**i**-push

Na-break ng atleta ang rekord. = *The athlete was able to break the record.*
I-push mo na ang mga plano mo. = *Push for your plans.*

-UM-

ENGLISH VERB	PAST	PRESENT	FUTURE	IMPERATIVE
park	p**um**ark	p**um**a-park	**pa**-park	p**um**ark
party	p**um**arty	p**um**a-party	**pa**-party	p**um**arty

P<u>u</u>mark ka na lang sa tabi. = *Just <u>park</u> on the side.*
Gabi-gabi p<u>u</u>ma-party si Gabriel. = *Gabriel <u>parties</u> every night.*

-IN-

ENGLISH VERB	PAST	PRESENT	FUTURE	IMPERATIVE
bake	b<u>in</u>ake	b<u>in</u>e-bake	<u>i</u>be-bake	<u>i</u>-bake
fold	f<u>in</u>old	f<u>in</u>o-fold	<u>i</u>fo-fold	<u>i</u>-fold

B<u>in</u>ake ni Suzy ang tinapay. = *Suzy <u>baked</u> the bread.*
<u>I</u>-fold mo ang mga napkin. = *<u>Fold</u> the napkins.*

I-

ENGLISH VERB	PAST	PRESENT	FUTURE	IMPERATIVE
greet	<u>i</u>ginreet	<u>i</u>gini-greet	<u>i</u>gi-greet	<u>i</u>-greet
bash	<u>i</u>binash	<u>i</u>bina-bash	<u>i</u>ba-bash	<u>i</u>-bash

<u>I</u>-greet mo si Nash ng "Happy Birthday". = *<u>Give</u> Nash a "Happy Birthday" greeting.*
Ibinash ng mga tagasuporta ni Angelina Jolie ang mga paparazzi. = *Angelina Jolie's fans <u>bashed</u> the paparazzis.*

So, why is it important to know how to conjugate English verbs with Tagalog affixes? As you learn the language, you will realize how common it is to hear English words in native conversations. In some cases, the English counterpart is considered the natural way of saying something, rather than its Tagalog equivalent.

For example, the verb *break* or in Tagalog, **bali**. From the sample sentence **Na-break ng atleta ang rekord** *(The athlete was able to break the record)*, it is more natural to say **na-break** instead of **nabali**. Using its Tagalog counterpart will make you sound too formal or too unnatural.

As a general rule though, context is the most important thing to consider in using loanwords. While you can use Tagalog affixes with most English verbs, some of the words may end up looking out of place when trying to formulate sentences. The key is to expose yourself to everyday conversations (watching movies, having a language partner, etc.) to catch which utterances sound natural and which sentence formulations don't work.

VERB AFFIXES + NOUNS

It is very common in Tagalog to attach verb affixes to nouns to signify the action most related to it.

Examples:

Nagtren ako papunta sa Tokyo. = *I went on a train/rode a train to get to Tokyo.* (Noun: **tren**)
Magkakanin ka ba? = *Will you eat rice?* (Noun: **kanin**)
Nag-apoy ang uling. = *The charcoal caught flames/fire.* (Noun: **apoy**)
Nagdoktor ako kahapon. = *I went to see a doctor yesterday.* (Noun: **doktor**)

Now, another common affix added to nouns is **magka-**. This affix is short for **magkaroon ng** which *means to have or to be in possession of something.*

Examples:

Nagkakanser ako limang taon na ang nakalipas. = *I had cancer five years ago.* (Noun: **kanser**)
Magkakakotse din ako balang araw. = *Someday I will own a car too.* (Noun: **kotse**)
Nagkaanak siya sa Amerika. = *She had (gave birth to) her child in America.* (Noun: **anak**)
Nagkabahay akong sarili noong tatlumpung taong gulang na ako. =
I was 30 years old when I had my own house. (Noun: **bahay**)

EXERCISE #3

Piliin ang tamang pangngalan o hiram na salita upang mabuo ang pandiwa.
Choose the correct noun or loanword to form the verb.

_____ 1. Mag-_____ ka para sagutan ang iyong takdang-aralin.
(Use a _____ to complete your homework.)

    a. glass   **b.** ballpoint pen   **c.** electric fan

_____ 2. Nag-_____ ako papunta dito. *(I rode a _____ to get here.)*

    a. bus   **b.** bird   **c.** rope

_____ 3. Si Shiela ay nagka-_____ kaya binati ko siya.
(Shiela got a/an _____ so I congratulated her.)

    a. cancer   **b.** award   **c.** problem

_____ 4. Mag-_____ tayo pagkatapos magtrabaho. *(Let's get _____ after work.)*

    a. cat   **b.** movie   **c.** coffee

_____ 5. Nagka _____ siya dahil masipag siya.
(She was able to get a house because she is hardworking.)

    a. bahay   **b.** aso   **c.** kotse

_____ 6. Magkaka _____ pa kaya ako? *(Will I still be able to find a husband/wife?)*

    a. kaibigan   **b.** nanay   **c.** asawa

_____ 7. Na _____ ako ngayong araw! *(I was on the news today!)*

    a. balita   **b.** doktor   **c.** pulis

_____ 8. Mag _____ ka na lang papunta sa probinsya.
(Just ride a boat to get to the province.)

    a. eroplano   **b.** bangka   **c.** sasakyan

MODIFYING TAGALOG VERBS

Now that you know the important affixes used to conjugate Tagalog verbs, it's time to learn their modifiers. Just like English, there are different types of adverbs in Tagalog:

ADVERB OF TIME

An adverb of time (**pang-abay na pamanahon**) indicates when the action occurs, for how long, and how frequently. This adverb can appear before or after the verb.

noon – *then*
sa – *on/in*
mula – *from/since*
hanggang – *until*
kapag/kung/nang – *when*

nakaraan – *last/ago*
kanina – *a while ago/earlier*
mamaya – *later*
bukas – *tomorrow*
kahapon – *yesterday*

ngayon – *now*
kaagad – *immediately*
tuwing/kada – *whenever/every*
sa susunod – *next*

Examples:

Maglalaba bukas si ate. = *My older sister will wash clothes tomorrow.*
Umalis kaagad ang estudyante pagkatapos ng klase. = *The student immediately left after the class.*
Maghihintay ako hanggang sa susunod na linggo. = *I will wait until next week.*
Si Sarah ay aalis mamayang gabi. = *Sarah will leave (later) tonight.*
Naghahanda tuwing Pasko ang aming pamilya. = *Our family prepares food every Christmas.*
Mula pagkabata ay kumakanta na ako. = *I have been singing since I was a child.*
Bumili ako noong Sabado ng sapatos. = *I bought shoes last Saturday.*

Instead of using **kada/tuwing**, we can also reduplicate an adverb to mean *every*.

Gabi-gabing nagdarasal ang bata. = *The child prays every night.*
Nagpupunta siya sa Maynila buwan-buwan. = *He/She goes to Manila every month.*
Minu-minuto kitang iniisip. = *I think of you every minute.*

ADVERB OF PLACE

An adverb of place (**pang-abay na panlunan**) signifies the place where the action is taking place. The place is usually preceded by the word **sa** + place. If the action is at a person's place/house, you can use the word **kina** + the person's name. Just like the adverb of time, this adverb also appears before or after the verb.

sa taas/ibabaw – *above*
sa baba/ilalim – *below*
sa tabi – *beside*
sa labas – *outside*
sa loob – *inside*
sa harap – *in front*

sa likod – *at the back*
sa malapit – *nearby*
sa malayo – *far*
sa gitna – *in the middle*
dito – *here*
doon – *there*

Examples:
<u>Tumalon</u> sa <u>ibabaw</u> ng <u>sasakyan</u> ang pusa. = *The cat <u>jumped on top of the car</u>.*
Si Ella ay <u>bibisita kina Jacob</u>. = *Ella <u>will visit Jacob's place</u>.*
<u>Lumapit</u> ka <u>dito</u>. = *<u>Come here</u>.*
<u>Naglalaro sa tabi ng daan</u> ang mga bata. = *The kids <u>are playing on the roadside</u>.*
<u>Pumasok sa loob</u> ang aso. = *The dog <u>went inside</u>.*
<u>Pupunta ka ba kina Christine</u>? = *Are you <u>going</u> to <u>Christine's place</u>?*
<u>Huminto sa gitna ng kalsada</u> ang motor. = *The motorcycle <u>stopped in the middle of the road</u>.*

ADVERB OF DEGREE

An adverb of degree **(pang-abay na pang-antas)** shows the intensity/intention of the action. This adverb usually appears before the verb, except for **yata**.

medyo – *a little*
siguro/baka – *maybe*
tila/yata/parang/mukha – *seemingly*
malamang – *most likely*
marahil – *probably*

talaga – *really*
sadya – *just/simply*
sigurado – *certainly*
tunay – *truly*

Examples:
<u>Medyo nagalit</u> si George sa nangyari. = *George <u>got a little angry</u> over what happened.*
<u>Siguradong uulan</u> nang malakas mamaya. = *It <u>will surely rain hard</u> later.*
<u>Napagod yata</u> si Lola sa pagtakbo. = *Grandma <u>seems to have gotten tired</u> from running.*
<u>Tila natatakot</u> ang bata sa palabas. = *It looks like the kid <u>is getting scared</u> from the show.*
<u>Sadyang nagtatampo</u> lang si Inay. = *Mom <u>is just really upset</u>.*

ADVERB OF MANNER

An adverb of manner **(pang-abay na pamamaraan)** indicates the way an action is done. It follows the formula: *verb* + **nang** + *adverb*.

nang mabilis – *quickly*
nang marahan – *gently/slowly*
nang malakas – *loudly*
nang madali – *easily*
nang maayos – *properly*

nang mabuti – *carefully*
nang mahigpit – *tightly*
nang seryoso – *seriously*
nang mapayapa – *peacefully*
nang paulit-ulit – *repeatedly*

Examples:
Mag-isip ka nang mabuti. = *Think carefully.*
Nagmamaneho nang marahan si Itay. = *Dad is driving slowly.*
Sagutin mo nang seryoso ang mga tanong. = *Answer the questions seriously.*
Umiyak nang paulit-ulit ang bata. = *The child cried repeatedly.*
Natapos nang mapayapa ang protesta. = *The protest ended peacefully.*

Another pattern that you can follow with adverbs of manner is *adverb* + **na**, **-ng**, **-g** + *verb*.

NA

We use **na** when the adverb ends with a consonant.

Paulit-ulit na umiyak ang bata. = *The child cried repeatedly.*
Mabilis na natapos ang pulong. = *The meeting ended quickly.*

-NG

We attach the affix **-ng** to adverbs that end with a vowel.

Mapayapang natapos ang protesta. = *The protest ended peacefully.*
Masusing inimbistagahan ng pulis ang kaso. = *The police investigated the case scrupulously.*

-G

We attach the affix **-g** to adverbs that end with the letter **n**.

Marahang nagmamaneho si itay. = *Dad is driving slowly.*
Madamdaming nagpaalam ang pangulo. = *The president emotionally bid goodbye.*

NG VS. NANG

It is critical to not confuse the noun article **ng** and adverb marker **nang** *(-ly)* when dealing with Tagalog verbs. While both words appear after a verb, **ng** precedes the object of the action while **nang** signifies the manner in which the action is done.

In essence, **ng** works as an object marker that tends to be placed before the noun as prepositions would be in English. It also works as a possessive marker to indicate objects that are indefinite.

Nang, on the other hand, works as an adverb marker, a conjunction that connects two adjectives or verbs, or as a conjunction of "when" in a subordinate clause.

Examples:
Si Brian ay kumain ng mangga. = *Brian ate a mango.*
Si Brian ay kumain nang mabilis. = *Brian ate quickly.*

Naglalaro ng basketbol ang bata. = *The child is playing basketball.*
Naglalaro nang masaya ang bata. = *The child is playing happily.*

Naglinis ng bahay si ate. = *My older sister cleaned the house.*
Naglinis nang padabog si ate. = *My older sister cleaned agitatedly.*

EXERCISE #4

Kumpletuhin ang sanaysay sa pamamagitan ng pagsulat ng angkop na salita sa patlang.
Complete the following passage by writing the correct word in the blank.

medyo	paulit-ulit	mabilis	maglilinis
bumili	nagpunta	niluto	kumain
bibisita	gabi		

ika-12 ng Hunyo, 2021

Dear Diary,

_____ ako kanina sa palengke.

_____ ako ng isda, karne, at mga gulay. Pagdating ko sa bahay ay _____ na ni inay ang ulam para sa pananghalian. _____ kami nang _____ dahil _____ pa kami ng bahay. Mamayang _____ kasi ay _____ ang aming mga kamag-anak. Winalis ko nang _____ ang aming sahig. _____ napagod ako sa paglilinis kaya nagpahinga na din ako pagkatapos.

June 12, 2021

Dear Diary,

I went to the market earlier. I bought fish, meat, and vegetables. When I got home, mom immediately cooked our dish for lunch. We ate quickly because we're still going to clean the house. My relatives will visit tonight. I swept the floor repeatedly. I got a little bit tired so I took some rest after everything.

LISTENING #1

Makinig at tukuyin kung ang pandiwa ay nasa anyong nakalipas, kasalukuyan o hinaharap.
Listen to each sentence and identify if the verb is in the past, present or future tense.

1. _____
2. _____
3. _____
4. _____
5. _____
6. _____
7. _____
8. _____
9. _____
10. _____

B. VOCABULARY

This section provides 60 very useful verbs that will enrich your Tagalog vocabulary. You will learn to express your daily activities, your feelings/state, your travel, and so much more.

DAILY ACTIVITIES

ROOT VERB	PAST	PRESENT	FUTURE	IMPERATIVE
1) tulog – to sleep	natulog	natutulog	matutulog	matulog
2) gising – to wake up	nagising	nagigising	magigising	gumising
3) kain – to eat	kumain	kumakain	kakain	kumain
4) inom – to drink	uminom	umiinom	iinom	uminom
5) luto – to cook	nagluto	nagluluto	magluluto	magluto
6) bihis – to get dressed	nagbihis	nagbibihis	magbibihis	magbihis
7) pahinga – to rest	nagpahinga	nagpapahinga	magpapahinga	magpahinga
8) nood – to watch	nanood	nanonood	manonood	manood
9) tayo – to stand up	tumayo	tumatayo	tatayo	tumayo
10) upo – to sit	umupo	umuupo	uupo	umupo
11) higa – to lie down	humiga	humihiga	hihiga	humiga
12) ligo – to take a bath	naligo	naliligo	maliligo	maligo
13) sipilyo – to brush one's teeth	nagsipilyo	nagsisipilyo	magsisipilyo	magsipilyo
14) suklay – to comb one's hair	nagsuklay	nagsusuklay	magsusuklay	magsuklay
15) ehersisyo – to exercise	nag-ehersisyo	nag-eehersisyo	mag-eehersisyo	mag-ehersisyo

Examples:

Magsipilyo ka bago matulog. = <u>Brush</u> your teeth before sleeping.
Nanonood ang aming pamilya ng telebisyon. = Our family <u>is watching</u> the television.
Uminom ka na ba ng gatas? = <u>Did</u> you <u>drink</u> your milk already?
Gumising ka nang maaga bukas. = <u>Wake</u> up early tomorrow.
Hihiga lang ako saglit. = I <u>will</u> just <u>lie down</u> for a bit.

AT SCHOOL

ROOT VERB	PAST	PRESENT	FUTURE	IMPERATIVE
16) aral – to study	nag-aral	nag-aaral	mag-aaral	mag-aral
17) sulat – to write	nagsulat	nagsusulat	magsusulat	magsulat
18) basa – to read	nagbasa	nagbabasa	magbabasa	magbasa
19) turo – to teach	nagturo	nagtuturo	magtuturo	magturo
20) isip – to think	nag-isip	nag-iisip	mag-iisip	mag-isip
21) tanong – to ask	nagtanong	nagtatanong	magtatanong	magtanong
22) sagot – to answer	sumagot	sumasagot	sasagot	sumagot
23) pinta – to paint	nagpinta	nagpipinta	magpipinta	magpinta
24) kinig – to listen	nakinig	nakikinig	makikinig	makinig
25) tahimik – to keep quiet	tumahimik	tumatahimik	tatahimik	tumahimik

Examples:

Nag-aaral ang mga estudyante. = The students <u>are studying</u>.
Magtanong ka sa guro. = <u>Ask</u> the teacher.
Magbabasa ako ng libro sa silid-aklatan. = I <u>will read</u> a book at the library.
Sumagot ang bata sa katanungan ng guro. = The child <u>answered</u> the teacher's question.
Nagtuturo ka ba ng Ingles? = <u>Are</u> you <u>teaching</u> English?

AT THE OFFICE

ROOT VERB	PAST	PRESENT	FUTURE	IMPERATIVE
26) trabaho – to work	nagtrabaho	nagtatrabaho	magtatrabaho	magtrabaho
27) tawag – to call	tumawag	tumatawag	tatawag	tumawag
28) gawa – to carry out something	ginawa	ginagawa	gagawain/ gagawin	gawain/ gawin
29) utos – to command	nag-utos	nag-uutos	mag-uutos	mag-utos
30) simula – to start	nagsimula	nagsisimula	magsisimula	magsimula

Examples:

Nagtatrabaho si itay sa isang malaking kumpanya. = *My dad is working at a big company.*
Tumawag ka sa opisina. = *Call the office.*
Pakiusap, **gawin** mo ang iyong trabaho. = *Please, do your job.*

LEISURE ACTIVITIES/HOBBIES

ROOT VERB	PAST	PRESENT	FUTURE	IMPERATIVE
31) langoy – to swim	lumangoy	lumalangoy	lalangoy	lumangoy
32) takbo – to run	tumakbo	tumatakbo	tatakbo	tumakbo
33) kanta – to sing	kumanta	kumakanta	kakanta	kumanta
34) sayaw – to dance	nagsayaw	nagsasayaw	magsasayaw	magsayaw
35) tula – to recite a poem	tumula	tumutula	tutula	tumula

Examples:

Tutula ka ba sa harap ng maraming tao? = *Will you recite a poem in front of a large audience?*
Nagsasayaw ang mga bata. = *The kids are dancing.*
Pakiusap, **kumanta** ka mamaya. = *Please sing later.*

One important thing to note when expressing hobbies or leisure activities is that their English counterparts are generally used. These verbs usually take the **mag-** affixes.

Examples:

Nag-swimming kami kahapon. = *We went swimming yesterday.*
Mag-shopping ka para sumaya ka. = *Go shopping to feel better.*
Nag-jogging si Elisa kaninang umaga. = *Elisa went jogging this morning.*
Nag-ski sila kagabi. = *They went skiing last night.*
Magta-travel ako sa aking bakasyon. = *I will go traveling on my break.*

Additionally, it is also common to add Tagalog verb affixes to English nouns to express an action. It usually means *to use/play/make/eat/go* to the said noun.

Examples:
Nag-beach kami noong nakaraang taon. = *We went to the beach last year.*
Magpa-piano ako mamaya. = *I will play the piano later.*
Nag-football sila kahapon sa eskwelahan. = *They played football at school yesterday.*
Mag-spaghetti tayo mamaya. = *Let's cook spaghetti later.*
Nag-beer lang kami kagabi. = *We just drank beer last night.*

Remember the affix **magka-** which means "*to have*"? It is a common affix attached to English nouns too.

Examples:
Magkaka-diploma na ako sa Hunyo. = *I will have my diploma in June.*
Nagka-malaria si Itay. = *Dad contracted malaria.*
Magkaka-baby na kami. = *We will be having a baby.*
Nagka-business ang aming pamilya ngayong taon. = *Our family started a business this year.*
Magkaka-salary increase ang lahat ng empleyado. = *All employees will receive a salary increase.*

OTHER COMMON ENGLISH VERBS/NOUNS THAT YOU CAN USE WITH TAGALOG AFFIXES:

SPORTS	MUSICAL INSTRUMENTS	FOOD	ELECTRONICS
volleyball, soccer, bowling, golf, skating, billiards	violin, drums, flute, ukulele, piano, tambourine	burger, fries, chicken, coffee, pizza, beer	laptop, cellphone, computer, earphones, keyboard, screen
CORPORATE	**CULINARY**	**EDUCATION**	**COMMON ACTIVITIES**
meeting, conference, seminar, lecture, resign, apply, recruit	bake, microwave, defrost, mince, oven, grill, icing	college, research, report, thesis, enroll, drop, scholar	drive, paint, bike, shopping, gym, mall, commute

Any name of a place can also be attached to a Tagalog verb affix **(mag-)** to signify that the subject went, is going, or will go there. Note the hyphen that separates the affix in the written form.

Examples:

Magja-Japan kami ngayong Setyembre. = We <u>will go to Japan</u> this September.
Nag-club si Joan at Beth kagabi. = Joan and Beth <u>went to a club</u> last night.
Mag-Manila ka na lang sa kolehiyo. = <u>Just go to Manila</u> for college.
Nag-Harvard siya. = He/She <u>went to/studied at Harvard</u>.
Magdi-Disneyland kami bukas. = We <u>will go to Disneyland</u> tomorrow.

Note that when reduplicating the first syllable of an English word for present and future tenses, it is spelled how it sounds. Since we follow how the first syllable is pronounced, it does not necessarily reflect the original spelling. Examples:

beach	violin	sale (to go on sale)	trespass
nagbi-beach	**nagba-violin**	**nagse-sale**	**nagte-trespass**
magbi-beach	**magba-violin**	**magse-sale**	**magte-trespass**

FEELINGS/STATE

ROOT VERB	PAST	PRESENT	FUTURE	IMPERATIVE
36) luksa – to grieve	nagluksa	nagluluksa	magluluksa	magluksa
37) mahal – to love	nagmahal	nagmamahal	magmamahal	magmahal
38) saya – to have fun	nagsaya	nagsasaya	magsasaya	magsaya
39) lungkot – to be lonely	nalungkot	nalulungkot	malulungkot	malungkot
40) bato – to get bored	nabato	nababato	mababato	mabato
41) kaba – to get nervous	kinabahan	kinakabahan	kakabahan	kabahan
42) duda – to doubt	nagduda	nagdududa	magdududa	magduda
43) gana – to get motivated/to be driven	ginanahan	ginaganahan	gaganahan	ganahan
44) taka – to wonder	nagtaka	nagtataka	magtataka	magtaka
45) lito – to be confused	nalito	nalilito	malilito	malito
46) baliw – to be crazy	nabaliw	nababaliw	mababaliw	mabaliw
47) awa – to pity	naawa	naaawa	maaawa	maawa
48) suko – to give up	sumuko	sumusuko	susuko	sumuko
49) inis – to be annoyed	nainis	naiinis	maiinis	mainis
50) tukso – to be tempted	natukso	natutukso	matutukso	matukso

Examples:

Naiinis ako sa ginawa mo sa akin. = *I am annoyed* with what you did to me.
Huwag kang **malungkot** dahil lang sa sinabi niya. = *Don't be sad* over what he/she just said.
Nagluluksa si Jenny sa pagkamatay ng kaniyang aso. = *Jenny is grieving* over the death of her dog.
Natutukso ka ba na bilhin ang mamamahaling bag? = *Are you tempted* to buy the expensive bag?
Kinakabahan akong magreport mamaya. = *I am nervous* to report later.

PHYSICAL CONDITION/SENSATION

ROOT VERB	PAST	PRESENT	FUTURE	IMPERATIVE
51) gutom – *to be hungry*	nagutom	nagugutom	magugutom	magutom
52) pawis – *to sweat*	pinawisan	pinapawisan	papawisan	pawisan/ magpapawis
53) uhaw – *to be thirsty*	nauhaw	nauuhaw	mauuhaw	mauhaw
54) bulag – *to be blind*	nabulag	nabubulag	mabubulag	mabulag
55) bingi – *to lose one's hearing*	nabingi	nabibingi	mabibingi	mabingi
56) taba – *to gain weight*	tumaba	tumataba	tataba	tumaba/ magpataba
57) payat – *to lose weight*	pumayat	pumapayat	papayat	pumayat/ magpapayat
58) kiliti – *to feel ticklish*	nakiliti	nakikiliti	makikiliti	makiliti
59) lamig – *to feel cold*	nilamig	nilalamig	lalamigin	lamigin
60) init – *to feel hot*	nainitan	naiinitan	maiinitan	mainitan

Examples:

Naiinitan ako sa lugar na ito. = *I feel hot* in this place.
Hindi ka pa ba **nagugutom**? = *Aren't you hungry* yet?
Pinapawisan ako sa damit na ito. = *These clothes are making me sweat*.
Pumayat ako dahil sa pagkain ng masustansyang pagkain. = *I lost weight* from eating healthy food.
Lalamigin yata ako pagdating sa Hokkaido. = *I think I will get cold* when we arrive in Hokkaido.

EXERCISE #5

A. Isalin ang mga sumusunod na pangungusap.
Translate the following sentences.

DAILY ACTIVITIES

1. Your mother is sleeping.
   _____

2. Don't eat rice.
   _____

3. The boy is brushing his teeth.
   _____

4. I will exercise tomorrow.
   _____

5. Lie down on the bed.
   _____

AT SCHOOL

6. The teacher is teaching English now.
   _____

7. The girl is writing her name.
   _____

8. The students will read a book.
   _____

9. *Everyone in the class kept quiet.*

_____.

10. *Shane is asking his classmate about the quiz.*

_____.

AT THE OFFICE

11. *Are you working as a secretary?*

_____.

12. *Mr. Lim commanded me to do this.*

_____.

13. *I will do my job.*

_____.

LEISURE ACTIVITIES/HOBBIES

14. *The kids are singing.*

_____.

15. *Michael will recite a poem later.*

_____.

FEELINGS/STATE

16. *I am annoyed at you.*

_____.

17. *I will be sad when you leave.*

_____.

18. *Do you pity the neighbor's dog?*

_____

PHYSICAL CONDITION/SENSATION

19. *My friend is thirsty.*

_____

20. *I am sweating because I feel hot here.*

_____

B. Piliin ang tamang anyo ng pandiwang hiram sa Ingles.
Choose the correct verb form of the English loanwords.

_____ 1. _____ ako papuntang Maynila bukas. *(I will drive to Manila tomorrow.)*

a. Nag-drive   b. Nag-dadrive   c. Mag-dadrive   d. Mag-drive

_____ 2. _____ si Emily noong nakaraang buwan. *(Emily went to the beach last month.)*

a. Nag-beach   b. Nagbi-beach   c. Magbi-beach   d. Mag-beach

_____ 3. _____ ako para sa aking trabaho. *(I am using a laptop for my work.)*

a. Nag-laptop   b. Nagla-laptop   c. Magla-laptop   d. Mag-laptop

_____ 4. _____ ka ba sa Linggo? *(Will you bake on Sunday?)*

a. Nag-bake   b. Nagbe-bake   c. Magbe-bake   d. Mag-bake

_____ 5. _____ si Jaime sa akin kahapon. *(Jaime texted me yesterday.)*

a. Nag-text   b. Nagte-text   c. Magte-text   d. Mag-text

_____ 6. _____ ako habang nag-aaral. *(I got a migraine while studying.)*

a. Nagka-migraine   b. Nagkaka-migraine   c. Magkaka-migraine   d. Magka-migraine

_____ 7. _____ kami sa susunod na linggo. *(We will play football next week.)*

a. Nag-football   b. Nagfu-football   c. Magfu-football   d. Mag-football

_____ 8. _____ na ako sa wakas! *(I will get a promotion finally!)*

a. Nagka-promotion   b. Nagkaka-promotion
c. Magkaka-promotion   d. Magka-promotion

_____ 9. _____ sina Wally kagabi. *(Wally and his company drank tequila last night.)*

a. Nag-tequila   b. Nagte-tequila   c. Magte-tequila   d. Mag-tequila

_____ 10. _____ ka sa akin na hindi ka aalis. *(You promised me that you will not leave.)*

a. Nag-promise   b. Nagpa-promise   c. Magpa-promise   d. Mag-promise

 LISTENING #2

Makinig at guhitan ang damdaming ipinapahayag ng mga pandiwa.
Listen to the recording and underline the feelings expressed.

1. grieving   loving   wondering
2. grieving   loving   wondering
3. grieving   loving   wondering
4. annoyed   tempted   confused
5. annoyed   tempted   confused
6. annoyed   tempted   confused
7. will wonder   will doubt   will give up
8. will wonder   will doubt   will give up
9. will wonder   will doubt   will give up
10. will love   loving   loved

SECTION 6

TAYO'Y KUMAIN!
LET'S EAT!

Now that you've gotten this far, it's just about the right time to learn how to express your goals, aspirations, wants, and desires. And there's no better way to begin than through learning a topic close to many a Filipino's heart—food! Filipinos *adore* food. Food, drink, and merriment are part and parcel of Filipino culture, after all.

Apart from food and beverages, you'll also learn how to discern the rules between the many ways you can express your wants in Tagalog: through **dapat**, **gusto**, and other similar pseudo verbs.

WHAT ARE "PSEUDO VERBS"?

In English, modal verbs are verbs used to express needs or wants. These include the following examples: *must*, *shall*, *will*, *should*, *would*, *can*, *could*, *may*, and *might*.

In Tagalog, we have the *pseudo verbs*. *Pseudo verbs* indicates several modalities expressing obligations, desires, and wants typically expressed by modal verbs in English.

Now, where does the "*pseudo*" part come in, you might ask? Pseudo verbs, as the name implies, serve as "*false*" verbs that act a little different from regular verbs.

For instance, pseudo verbs do not use the typical affixes and markers found in Tagalog to indicate aspects. Moreover, pseudo verbs do not use affixes to determine what the sentence is emphasizing or focusing on.

Therefore, pseudo verbs are actually *easier* to use. In most cases, pseudo verbs don't need to be changed or modified. You simply use the root verb.

However, as the pseudo verb isn't a "full-fledged" verb, it is usually paired with a regular Tagalog verb. Take, for instance, the following example:

<u>**Kailangan**</u> kong <u>pumunta</u> sa palengke. = *I <u>need to go</u> to the market.*

Note that in this sentence, **"kailangan"** functions as a pseudo verb (meaning *necessary*), and the action of going to the market serves as the main verb. Also note how the mood changes by adding the pseudo verb. In this sentence, the subject is not actually present at the market, and has expressed that he or she would *need* to be at the market. Therefore, in this case, the pseudo verb **"kailangan"** demonstrates the *need* to go to the market, while leaving the possibility that the subject might *not* actually go.

Here are some of the most commonly-used pseudo verbs in Tagalog.

Gusto – *like/want*
Gusto kong **kumain** ng adobo. – *I want to eat adobo.*
Gusto kong **uminom** ng tubig. – *I want to drink water.*

Ayaw – *dislike / do not or does not want*
Ayaw niyang **kumain** ng karne ng baka. – *He dislikes eating beef.*
Ayaw kong **pumunta** diyan. – *I do not want to go there.*

Kailangan – *need*
Kailangan kitang **ipakita** sa embahada. – *I need you to show up at the embassy.*
Kailangan kong **bumili** ng gulay sa tindahan. – *I need to buy vegetables at the store.*

Pwede – *can*
Pwede ka bang **magluto** ng kanin para sa hapunan? – *Can you cook rice for dinner?*
Pwede ba tayong **ipagluto** ng tatay mo? – *Can your dad cook for us?*
Pwede kitang **dalhin** sa paborito mong kainan. – *I can take you to your favorite restaurant.*

Baka – *might*
Baka dalhin ko ang mga bata sa Jollibee. – *I might take the kids to Jollibee.*
Baka gumawa ako ng mainit na sopas ng manok mamaya. – *I might make hot chicken soup later.*
Baka ipagtimpla kita ng kape. – *I might fix you a cup of coffee.*

Dapat – *must*
Dapat mong **ibabad** ang liempo sa suka. – *You must soak the pork belly in vinegar.*
Dapat mo munang **hanguin** ang manok mula sa kawali. – *You must first take the chicken from the frying pan.*
Dapat ba tayong **mag-init** ng mantika? – *Must we heat the oil?*

TIP: Note the affix **-ng** that is appended to the end of each pronoun following a verb. You will also need to do this if the pronoun being appended to ends in a vowel or the letter "n".

VOCABULARY

TYPICAL FILIPINO ENTRÉES

Adobong manok – *Chicken braised in garlic, vinegar, soy sauce, and oil*
Nilagang baka – *Boiled beef*
Kare-kare – *Braised oxtail stew in peanut sauce*
Tinolang manok – *Native chicken soup in ginger, onions, and fish sauce*
Sinigang na baboy – *Pork in sour broth*
Leche flan – *Milk and egg custard*

FOOD ITEMS

karne – *meat*
baboy – *pork*
baka – *beef*
manok – *chicken*
isda – *fish*

gulay – *vegetables*
prutas – *fruits*
hipon – *shrimp*
sugpo – *prawn*
kanin – *cooked rice*

bigas – *uncooked rice*
ulam – *main entrée/viand*
sabaw – *broth*
panghimagas – *dessert*

COOKING METHODS

nilaga – *boiled*
inihaw – *grilled*
prito – *fried*
ginisa – *sautéed*
sinigang – *cooked in soured broth*
adobo – *cooked in vinegar, soy sauce, oil, and garlic*
sinampalukan – *cooked in tamarind*
tinola – *cooked in broth with ginger, onions, and fish sauce*

ADJECTIVES USED TO DESCRIBE FOOD

matamis – *sweet*
maalat – *salty*
maanghang – *spicy*
maasim – *sour*
mapait – *bitter*
mapakla – *tart*
tamis-anghang – *sweet and spicy*

MEALS OF THE DAY

agahan / almusal – *breakfast*
tanghalian – *lunch*
meryenda – *snack (usually eaten between lunch and dinner)*
hapunan – *dinner*

Now, let's put it all together!

EXERCISE #1

Piliin ang pang-uri na maglalarawan sa sumusunod na mga pagkain.
Choose the adjective that will describe the following food items.

A. matamis   B. maalat   C. maanghang   D. maasim   E. mapait

_____ 1. sorbetes *(ice cream)*   _____ 6. tuyo *(dried fish)*

_____ 2. sinigang *(sour broth)*   _____ 7. kalamansi *(calamansi)*

_____ 3. sili *(pepper)*   _____ 8. suriso *(sausage)*

_____ 4. ampalaya *(bitter melon)*   _____ 9. mustasa *(mustard greens)*

_____ 5. kendi *(candy)*   _____ 10. kimtsi *(kimchi)*

EXERCISE #2

Piliin ang tamang pangalan para sa mga pagkaing nakalarawn sa ibaba.
Choose the correct name for the food items illustrated below.

baboy	baka	isda	panghimagas	hipon
manok	gulay	prutas	kanin	sabaw

1.

_____

6.

_____

2.

7.

3.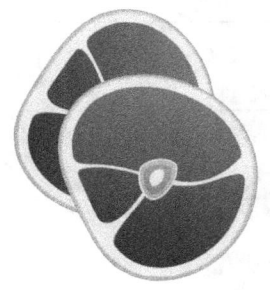

8.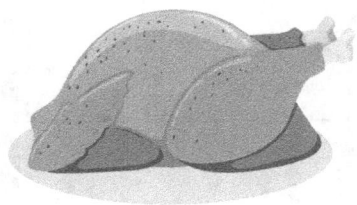

4.

9.

5.

10.

 **LISTENING #1**

Makinig at isulat ang paraan ng paglulutong binanggit.
Listen to the recording and identify the cooking methods used.

1. _____
2. _____
3. _____
4. _____
5. _____

Makinig at isulat ang pagkaing binanggit.
Listen to the recording and identify foods mentioned.

1. _____
2. _____
3. _____
4. _____
5. _____

SECTION 7

ANO ANG TRABAHO MO?
WHAT DO YOU DO?

Filipino culture is highly influenced by Western culture. Therefore, it should come as no surprise for foreigners to hear Filipinos code-switch between Tagalog and the rest of the Philippines' dialects, and foreign languages, mainly English, which is the lingua franca of business and higher education in the archipelago.

While most Filipinos speak English as the primary means of communication in corporate and business settings (and are in fact encouraged to do so), you'll find that you'll go a little farther by learning to speak Tagalog business phrases. Tagalog is, after all, still the main language spoken in the workplace within the National Capital Region. Moreover, talking about professions and occupations is one of the most common topics of conversation.

Thus, if you wish to converse with your colleagues, clients, and supervisors in Tagalog and build a rapport with them, learning basic Tagalog business phrases and how to talk about jobs, occupations, and professions will go a long way in your day-to-day interactions. Learning the right words and asking the right questions is helpful as you progress in your business or career.

GRAMMAR

Remember: In Tagalog, there is no equivalent form for expressing *"to be"*.

Therefore, the *"be"* verbs, such as *am*, *are*, or *is*, don't have literal translations in Tagalog. Instead, we would use **ay** or **ay mga** *(for plural nouns)* in the passive voice. In the spoken language, however, **ay** or **ay mga** is omitted entirely in favor of the pronoun. Have a look at the following examples.

Examples:
I am a translator. = **Ako ay tagapagsalin.**
I am a translator. = **Tagapagsalin ako.**

I am a doctor. = **Ako ay doktor.**
I am a doctor. = **Doktor ako.**

I am a lawyer. = **Ako ay abogado.**
I am a lawyer. = **Abogado ako.**

In essence, there is no verb that represents the *"be"* form in Tagalog. Easy.

VOCABULARY

These new Tagalog words about professions and jobs will open you to a world of new linguistic possibilities that allow you to structure more complex sentences. Soon, you'll be well on the way to progressing with your Tagalog.

The following table shows the most common professions available in the Tagalog language.

ENGLISH	TAGALOG
lawyer	abogado
student	estudyante/mag-aaral
architect	arkitekto
actor	aktor/artista
firefighter	bumbero
engineer	inhinyero
writer	manunulat
soldier	sundalo
businessperson	negosyante
doctor	doktor
nurse	nars
carpenter	karpintero
farmer	magsasaka
worker/laborer	manggagawa
mechanic	mekaniko
painter	pintor
pharmacist	parmasista
police officer	pulis
plumber	tubero
politician	politiko
mail carrier	kartero
agent (sales)	ahente
secretary	kalihim
tailor	mananahi
driver	tsuper
translator	tagapagsalin
veterinarian	beterinaryo
teacher	guro
scientist	siyentipiko

EXERCISE #1

Bilugan ang propesyon na makakatulong sa mga pangangailangang inilarawan dito.
Circle the profession that will help with the needs described.

1. May nasusunog na bahay sa aming pamayanan.
   There is a house burning in our community.

   a. abogado   b. doktor   c. bumbero

2. Ang bubungan ng tirahan ni Tiyo Jose ay kailangang kumpunihin.
   The roof of Uncle Jose's residence needs to be repaired.

   a. karpintero   b. nars   c. inhinyero

3. Paalis at may sasakyan siya, pero hindi siya marunong magmaneho.
   She's about to leave and has a vehicle, but she doesn't know how to drive.

   a. arkitekto   b. tsuper   c. pulis

4. Kailangan niyang magpatahi ng pantalon para sa dadaluhang kasalan.
   Trousers must be sewed for him to attend at a wedding ceremony.

   a. ahente   b. mananahi   c. kartero

5. Sino ang maaaring magtanggol sa pagdedemanda nila sa kaibigan ko?
   Who can defend my friend against their filed complaint?

   a. politiko   b. pintor   c. abogado

6. Pinatala ko na ang aking anak sa paaralan para magsimula nang matuto.
   I had my child enrolled in school already, for her to start learning.

   a. guro   b. beterinaryo   c. kalihim

7. Biglang naputol ang tubo ng tubig.
   The water pipe was suddenly cut.

   a. siyentipiko   b. aktor   c. tubero

8. Ang aming alagang aso ay may sakit.
   Our pet dog is sick.

   a. nars   b. beterinaryo   c. inhinyero

9. Siya ang nag-abot ng aking mga biniling gamot sa botika.
   He/she handed my the medicine I bought from the drugstore.

   a. parmasista   b. manunulat   c. sundalo

10. Siya ang nagdisenyo ng ipagagawang gusali.
    He designed the building to be constructed.

    a. bumbero   b. arkitekto   c. tagapagsalin

EXERCISE #2

Kumpletuhin ang mga pangungusap ng paglalarawan ng mga taong nasa ibaba.
Complete the descriptions of the people below.

1. Ako ay isang _____.

6. Ako ay isang _____.

2. Ako ay isang _____.

7. Ako ay isang _____.

3. Ako ay isang _____.

8. Ako ay isang _____.

4. Ako ay isang _____.

9. Ako ay isang _____.

5. Ako ay isang _____.

10. Ako ay isang _____.

 LISTENING #1

Makinig at isulat ang propesyon o trabahong binanggit.
Listen to the recording and identify the professions or jobs mentioned.

1. _____
2. _____
3. _____
4. _____
5. _____
6. _____
7. _____
8. _____
9. _____
10. _____

SECTION 8

ANO ANG MASASABI MO TUNGKOL SA...?
WHAT CAN YOU SAY ABOUT...?

Every language possesses subtle differences as far as expressing thoughts, emotions, and feelings. Novice Tagalog speakers don't necessarily have to grasp such abstract concepts from the get-go. However, if you wish to communicate in Tagalog with some measure of fluency, there are some verbs, phrases, and vocabulary that are perfectly adapted for when you need to get something off your chest.

Not to worry, however—by the end of this lesson, you'll have everything you need to adequately express yourself in Tagalog.

GRAMMAR

Filipinos are an expressive, demonstrative lot once you get to know them better. You may have found by now that Tagalog is also a deeply expressive language.

Whenever expressing thoughts and actions, Filipinos use the root words **isip**, **akala**, or **tila**, paired with a variety of verbs to indicate what they are doing, what they did, what they will do, and what they plan to do.

That said, let's get started with the basics.

TILA, AKALA, AND PALAGAY

In English, the verb form for *"to think"* can be expressed in these three words. These words all translate to *I think, He/She thinks, We/They think* whenever used in sentences. Let's take a look at their individual definitions as follows:

- **tila** – *an adverb expressing the phrase "it seems (that)"*
- **(sa) akala or (sa) palagay** – *a preposition indicating to have in mind or to think (literally translated as "in my mind")*

Let's learn to formulate sentences using these expressions.

Tila + *verb, adjective, or nominative pronoun*
(sa) + **palagay** + *possessive noun or pronoun*
(sa) + **akala** + *possessive noun or pronoun*

Tila is generally used at the beginning of a sentence in daily conversations, and expresses the speaker's own point of view.

Examples:
Tila uulan mamaya. = *It seems as though it will rain later.*
Tila nagkakamali siya. = *It seems he is mistaken.*
Ang sagot niya sa tanong mo ay tila makatotohanan. – *His answer to your question seems truthful.*

Meanwhile, **akala** and **palagay** (often with the particle "**sa**" at the beginning) are followed by either possessive nouns or pronouns.

Examples:
Sa akala ko, matapat kang bata. = *I think you're an honest kid.*
Sa akala nila, uuwi si Jose bukas. = *They think Jose is coming home tomorrow.*
Sa palagay ko, matatalo ang kandidato natin. = *I think our candidate will lose.*
Sa palagay ni Michael, ako ay maganda. = *Michael thinks I'm pretty.*

To Tagalog ears, sentences beginning with **(sa) akala** implies room for validation or contradiction as the speaker's own perceptions may be proven wrong in the end.

For instance, take the following sentence:

Sa akala ko, Pranses siya. = *I thought he was French.*

The example demonstrates how using **sa akala** negates the nationality of the subject as assumed by the speaker.

On the other hand, take the following example:

Sa palagay ko, nagkakamali ka. = *I think you're making a mistake.*

Sa palagay in this context expresses a personal opinion. In English, it's the equivalent of saying *"in my opinion..."*

ASKING FOR OPINIONS

Now that we've learned how to express opinions and thoughts, the next step is to learn how to ask what other Tagalog speakers think, if we wish to have natural-sounding Tagalog conversations and communicate in a much more effective manner.

Fortunately, it's as easy as formulating the most frequently used ways to ask for opinions, about anything under the sun.

Remember how we learned how to formulate questions in section 2? Well, it's just a matter of learning how to use conversation starters such as the following, and then adding the subject, pronoun, or noun.

Let's take a look at some of the most common ways Filipinos ask about opinions:

Ano ang masasabi mo (tungkol) sa...? = *What can you say about... ?*
Ano ang opinyon mo (tungkol) sa... = *What is your opinion about...?*
Ano ang tingin mo sa... = *What's your view on...?*

Note: In spoken Tagalog, the preposition *about* (or "**tungkol**") is often omitted for brevity. Moreover, the particle **ano ang** (or "*what is*") and **ano ang mga** (or "*what are*") are often contracted as **anong** or **anong mga**, respectively. It's no different from asking an English speaker "*What is up?*" or "*What's up?*" for starters.

Let's examine a few more examples using these three forms.

Examples
Ano ang masasabi mo tungkol sa paninigarilyo? = *What can you say about smoking?*
Ano ang opinyon mo tungkol sa presidente namin? = *What is your opinion about our president?*
Anong tingin mo sa gobyerno ng Estados Unidos? = *What's your view on the United States government?*
Anong masasabi mo sa panahon ngayong araw? = *What can you say about the weather today?*

Easy! It's all just a matter of putting it all together. Now, let's do some exercises.

 **EXERCISE #1**

Punan ang mga patlang ng "tila", "palagay", o "akala".
Fill in the blanks with "tila", "palagay", or "akala".

1. _____ didilim ang ulap ngayon.
   (It seems the cloud will become dark now.)

2. Sa _____ nila, matatalo sa laro ang pangkat pero hindi.
   (They thought the team would lose the game, but it didn't.)

3. Sa _____ ko, napapagod na ang anak ko.
   (I think my child is getting tired already.)

4. Sa _____ ni Alice, babayaran siya subalit tumakas ang nangutang sa kaniya.
   (Alice thought she would be paid but the debtor fled from her.)

5. _____ hindi pa matatapos ang pandemya.
   (It seems the pandemic will not end yet.)

6. Sa _____ ng may-ari, magiging matagumpay ang kaniyang negosyo.
   (The owner thinks his business will become successful.)

7. Sa _____ ni Teddy, malalaglag ang mga prutas pero nasa puno pa rin.
   (Teddy thought the fruits would fall but they are still on the tree.)

8. Si Inay ay _____ natutuwa sa aking tagumpay sa hanapbuhay.
   (Mom seems to be happy with my job success.)

9. Sa _____ ni Liza, maoospital siya subalit pinauuwi na siya ngayon.
   (Liza thinks she will be confined but she is being sent home now.)

10. Sa _____ namin, makakabawi ang ekonomiya ng ating bansa.
    (We think our country's economy will recover.)

 **LISTENING #1**

Makinig at isulat ang salitang nagpapahayag ng opinyon.
Listen to the recording and identify the words used to express opinions.

1. _____
2. _____
3. _____
4. _____
5. _____
6. _____
7. _____
8. _____
9. _____
10. _____

CONCLUSION

Thank you, and hooray for reaching the last portion of this workbook! Spending time reading the lessons and answering the exercises in each chapter paved the way for you to gain greater familiarity with Tagalog, and with the country where it is spoken.

As explained earlier, both the grammar and vocabulary lessons you have learned in this book clearly show the life and culture of those living in the Philippines. This workbook, for sure, has made you learn Tagalog not just as a mere language, but it helped you know the nation even more.

Specifically, the sections of this workbook enabled you to:

- learn the phonetics, orthography and loanwords. You discovered as well how places, directions, weather, numbers, months, dates, and days may be expressed.

- use politeness markers, basic greetings, and pronouns. You learned how to introduce and describe yourself by describing your nationality, work, age, family and hobbies. You likewise had the chance to ask questions, express your moods, emotions, and polite greetings.

- describe yourself better by detailing your physical traits, preferences, and personality.

- describe other people and things as well. You were also taught how to express your personal relationships, from those within your house to those in your community.

- focus on action by expressing a movement or an incident.

- communicate your goals, aspirations, wants, and desires. A fun way you learned is through Filipino food.

- express your thoughts, emotions, and feelings.

- have everything you need to adequately express yourself in Tagalog.

You may have just started but we are certain you won't get tired of learning even more. Keep going, keep learning and discover more Tagalog words!

And you deserve our warmest greetings – **Maligayang bati!**

ANSWER KEY

SECTION 1

Section 1 - Exercise #1

1. mayor
2. breakfast
3. administration
4. bicycle
5. bathroom
6. newspaper
7. accident
8. interview
9. kitchen
10. electricity
11. chemical
12. curtain
13. sink
14. circle of friends
15. nurse
16. plastic
17. police
18. cheat sheet
19. stand by
20. wise

Section 1 - Listening #1

1. aso
2. baka
3. bata
4. gusali
5. kalabaw
6. lima
7. nanay
8. relo
9. samba
10. tatay

Section 1 - Exercise #2

1. gitna
2. kanan
3. taas
4. kaliwa
5. baba

Section 1 - Exercise #3

A.
1. Enero
2. Pebrero
3. Marso
4. Abril
5. Mayo
6. Hunyo
7. Hulyo
8. Agosto
9. Setyembre
10. Oktubre
11. Nobyembre
12. Disyembre

B.
1. isa
2. dalawa
3. tatlo
4. apat
5. lima
6. anim
7. pito
8. walo
9. siyam
10. sampu

Section 1 - Exercise #4

1. **b.** maaraw
2. **b.** bagyo
3. **a.** mahangin
4. **c.** maulap
5. **a.** baha

Section 1 - Listening #2

Tumawag si Dennis sa kaibigang si Cathy para sa pagdiriwang ng kaniyang naalapit na kaarawan...

Dennis: Magandang gabi Cathy.

Cathy: Magandang gabi din naman Dennis. Bakit ka napatawag?

Dennis: Iimbitahin lang sana kita sa nalalapit kong kaarawan. Ikaapat ng hapon sa Taal Vista, Tagaytay.

Cathy: Naku, malapit na nga pala ang kaarawan. Sa Linggo, ika-labindalawa ng Hunyo, tama ba?

Dennis: Ang galing mo! Naalala mo pa.

Cathy: Siyempre naman, ikaw pa ba?

Dennis: O sige ha, aasahan ko ang iyong pagdalo.

Cathy: Oo naman, sasakay ako ng bus sa Pasay papuntang Tagaytay.

Dennis: Salamat at magkita tayo.

1. **c.** evening
2. **a.** 4 PM
3. **b.** Tagaytay
4. **b.** June 12
5. **a.** Sunday

SECTION 2

Section 2 - Exercise #1

1. B. "Magandang umaga."
2. A. "Maligayang Pasko!"
3. I. "Maligayang Kapistahan."
4. J. "Magandang tanghali."
5. C. "Maligayang Araw ng mga Puso."
6. D. "Maligayang Kaarawan."
7. H. "Maligayang pagbabalik."
8. G. "Maligayang Anibersaryo."
9. F. "Magandang gabi."
10. E. "Maligayang Bagong Taon."/ "Manigong Bagong Taon."

Section 2 - Exercise #2

1. siya
2. ko
3. sila
4. kita
5. kayo
6. akin
7. mo
8. kaniya
9. kami
10. ito

Section 2 - Listening #1

Recording:

1. Your father, who is an Overseas Filipino Worker (OFW), just came home. How do you say welcome home in Tagalog?

2. Your cousin just graduated from college. How would you congratulate him in Tagalog?

3. How do you say "have a prosperous new year in Tagalog"?

4. How do you greet your mother in Tagalog during dinnertime?

5. Identify the first person pronoun in this sentence: Ako ang bumili ng tinapay.

6. Identify the politeness word in this sentence: Si ate po ang naghatid kay Mara sa paaralan.

7. Ako, Ikaw, Sila. Which among these pronouns refer to second person?

8. How do you say I love you in Tagalog?

9. Identify the pronoun in this sentence: Pakiabot mo nga iyon.

10. In Tagalog, how do you say happy birthday to a friend?

Answers:

1. Maligayang pagbabalik!
2. Pagbati!
3. Manigong Bagong Taon
4. Magandang gabi!
5. Ako.
6. Po
7. Ikaw
8. Mahal Kita!
9. iyon
10. Maligayang kaarawan!

Section 2 - Exercise #3

A.
1. Amerika
2. Koreya
3. Hapon
4. Pilipinas
5. Inglatera
6. Espanya
7. Italya
8. Portugal

B.
1. Ako ay guro.
2. Siya ay doktor.
3. Mahilig ako magluto.
4. Mahilig siya kumanta.
5. Ako ay abogado.
6. Ako ang bunso.
7. Galing ako sa malaking pamilya.
8. Paborito ko ang pangingisda.
9. Paborito ko ang pag-akyat ng bundok.
10. Ako ay dalawampung taong gulang.

C.
1. malungkot
2. galit
3. nagulat
4. malungkot
5. masaya
6. malungkot
7. nagulat
8. masaya
9. malungkot
10. galit

Section 2 - Exercise #4

1. Sino
2. Saan
3. Magkano
4. Paano
5. Kumusta
6. Kailan
7. Alin
8. Kanino
9. Bakit
10. Ano

Section 2 - Listening #2

Recording:

Magandang umaga sa lahat lalo na sa ating mahal na guro Binibining Miranda. Ako po si Mark Abella na isang Bulakenyo. Ang tatay ko po na isang abogado ay Manilenyo, habang ang aking ina na isang mananahi ay Bulakenya. Ako po ay labing-anim na taong gulang at mayroon dalawang kapatid. Inuubos ko ang aking libreng oras sa panonood ng sine, pagtugtog ng gitara at paglalakad sa kabukiran. Kapag may sobrang pera, gusto ko rin ang paglalakbay. Kabado man ako sa aking unang araw sa paaralang ito, ako pa rin ay sabik sa mga bagong matutunan at mararanasan. Komportable at may tiwala ako sa aking sarili kaya alam kong marami akong magiging bagong kaibigan.

1. Binibining Miranda
2. Bulakenyo / Bulacan
3. Manilenyo / Manila
4. mananahi
5. dalawa
6. labing-anim na taong gulang
7. paglalakbay
8. abogado
9. kabado
10. komportable

SECTION 3

Section 3 - Exercise #1

1. **ang** aso
2. **si** John
3. **ng** eroplano
4. **ang** simbahan
5. **'yung** doktor
6. **sina** Steve at Jake
7. **si** Papa
8. **'yung** klase
9. **ng** regalo
10. **ang** mga sapatos

Section 3 - Exercise #2

1. hindi masaya
2. mas maganda kaysa kay Jennie
3. fat dog
4. huwag/'wag mag-aral
5. walang pera
6. no doctor
7. kindest
8. pinakamainit
9. more delicious
10. huwag magsalita

Section 3 - Listening #1

Recording:

Ngayong araw na ito, ako ay nakatanggap ng pinakamagagandang regalo. Binigyan ako ni nanay ng relo. Nagpuntahan ang aking mga kaibigan sa aming bahay. Binigyan nila ako ng mga damit at mga sapatos bilang regalo. Maraming prutas ang aking mga hinanda. Mayroon akong mga mansanas, mga ubas at mga saging. Nagkaroon din ng mga palaro para pampalipas ng oras. Walang kinatatakutan ang aking mga kaibigan, kaya naging puro kasiyahan lang ang aking kaarawan. Alam kong mas masaya ang aking pagdiriwang ngayong taon kaysa noong nakaraan.

1. pinakamagaganda
2. relo
3. mga kaibigan
4-5. mga damit, mga sapatos
6-8. mga mansanas, mga ubas at mga saging
9. walang kinatatakutan
10. mas masaya

Section 3 - Exercise #3

A.
1. F. ulo
2. J. mata
3. H. tainga
4. A. labi
5. D. kamay
6. B. buhok
7. C. paa
8. E. braso
9. G. ilong
10. I. binti

B.
1. c. matigas
2. b. mahaba
3. a. bilugan
4. b. luma
5. a. morena
6. b. makapal
7. c. matulis
8. b. maiksi
9. a. malaki
10. b. malambot

Section 3 - Exercise #4

1. nakakatawa
2. mapagkumbaba
3. pasensyoso
4. mapagparaya
5. mapagbigay
6. palakaibigan
7. kuripot
8. magalang
9. mainitin ang ulo
10. strikto

Section 3 - Exercise #5

A.
1. dilaw
2. berde
3. asul
4. pula
5. itim

B.
1. H. pagsusulat
2. F. paggigitara
3. A. pagbibisikleta
4. B. pagkuha ng litrato
5. D. pag-inom ng tsaa
6. C. pagkain ng matatamis
7. I. pag-aalaga ng bata
8. G. pagkanta
9. E. pagtulong sa kapwa
10. J. pagtuturo

Section 3 - Listening #2

Recording:

Ang sanggol na isinilang ni Maica ay mayroong bilugang mukha at matabang pisngi. Nakakatuwang pagmasdan ang kaniyang matangos na ilong at mapulang labi. Masasabing gwapo ang sanggol na mayroon morenong balat at maitim na buhok.

1. bilugan
2. mataba
3. moreno
4. matangos
5. maitim

Recording:

Masaya at may respeto sa isa't isa ang pamilya ni Pedro. Ang kaniyang ama ay strikto. Hindi rin maikakaila ang pagiging masipag nito sa trabaho. Ang kaniyang ina naman ay pasensyosa. Ito ay madalas tahimik lang. Pinapakita ni Pedro ang pagiging magalang niya sa pamamagitan ng laging pagsasabi ng po at opo. Isa siyang masikap na mag-aaral.

6. masikap
7. pasensyosa
8. strikto
9. masipag
10. magalang

SECTION 4

Section 4 - Exercise #1

1. a little sensitive
2. a little red
3. very tall
4. really cheerful
5. very fat
6. a little smooth/slippery
7. too handsome
8. very yellow
9. very snob
10. a little lively

Section 4 - Exercise #2

1. **c.** taga-
2. **b.** ka-
3. **a.** pang-
4. **b.** tag-
5. **a.** -han
6. **a.** ka- -an
7. **a.** taga-
8. **b.** pang-
9. **c.** ka-
10. **a.** -an

Section 4 - Exercise #3

1. **F.** ito
2. **D.** daw
3. **H.** na
4. **B.** nandito
5. **C.** nga
6. **G.** doon
7. **E.** sana
8. **A.** muna
9. **I.** pala
10. **J.** nandiyan

Section 4 - Listening #1

Recording:

Masyadong emosyonal ang palabas sa telebisyon. Madilim-dilim ang paligid at kasalukuyang pinapakita ang isang ubod ng payat na babae na tila malapit ng malagutan ng hininga. Paulit-ulit niyang binabanggit ang pangalan ng napakatalino niyang anak. Malungkot ang tugtog na naririnig habang umaagos ang luha sa mga mata ng matanda.

1. **a.** masyadong emosyonal
2. **c.** ubod ng payat
3. **b.** napakatalino
4. **a.** madilim-dilim
5. **b.** malungkot

Section 4 - Exercise #4

A. 1. pari
    2. pangulo/presidente
    3. sundalo
    4. dentista
    5. arkitekto
    6. musikero
    7. weyter
    8. drayber

B. b. sundalo
    c. matulungin
    a. masisipag
    b. sweldo
    c. populado
    a. gobyerno
    b. kusina
    b. pari
    c. bise presidente
    a. kumpanya

Section 4 - Listening #2

Recording:

1. Malayo ang palengke sa bahay ko.
2. Malapit ang paaralan sa bahay ko.
3. Si Teddy Arevallo ang kapitan ng Barangay Poblacion.
4. Si Mark Cruz ang pangunahing kagawad sa Barangay Poblacion.
5. Si Rodrigo Duterte ang ikalabing-anim na pangulo ng Pilipinas.
6. Ang ikalabing-anim na pangalawang pangulo ng Pilipinas ay si Leni Robredo.
7. Ang Pilipinas ay mayroong dalawampu't apat na mga senador.
8. Bawat bayan ay mayroon isang alcalde.
9. Maraming pabrika sa Laguna.
10. Malalaking korporasyon ang makikita sa Makati.

1. b. school
2. a. Teddy Arevallo
3. b. Leni Robredo
4. b. mayor
5. b. Makati

SECTION 5

Section 5 - Exercise #1

A. **Mag-**
1. nag-aalay
2. nagsabi
3. magsasabi
4. nagpaalam
5. nagpapaalam

Ma-
6. namamanhid
7. mamamanhid
8. nalito
9. nabuhat
10. mabubuhat

-Um-
11. aalis
12. bumababa
13. pumalpak
14. papalpak

-In-
15. pinipilit
16. pipilitin
17. minithi
18. kinakain
19. kakainin

I-
20. ikinabit
21. ikakabit
22. isinama
23. isinasama
24. isinusulat
25. isusulat

B.
1. sigaw
2. tawa
3. sulat/aral
4. kain
5. lakad
6. yakap
7. laro

Section 5 - Exercise #2

1. **a.** nagbayad
2. **a.** kakagising
3. **b.** ikinalungkot
4. **a.** manghalik
5. **c.** kumain
6. **a.** maglalakad
7. **a.** ipambabayad
8. **b.** nabasa
9. **b.** nagpunta
10. **a.** sasama

Section 5 - Exercise #3

1. **b.** ballpoint pen
2. **a.** bus
3. **b.** award
4. **c.** coffee
5. **a.** bahay
6. **c.** asawa
7. **a.** balita
8. **b.** bangka

Section 5 - Exercise #4

Dear Diary,

Nagpunta ako kanina sa palengke. **Bumili** ako ng isda, karne, at mga gulay. Pagdating ko sa bahay ay **niluto** na ni inay ang ulam para sa pananghalian. **Kumain** kami nang **mabilis** dahil **maglilinis** pa kami ng bahay. Mamayang **gabi** kasi ay **bibisita** ang aming mga kamag-anak. Winalis ko nang **paulit-ulit** ang aming sahig. **Medyo** napagod ako sa paglilinis kaya nagpahinga na din ako pagkatapos.

Section 5 - Listening #1

1. Mamahalin kita. — future / hinaharap
2. Naglinis siya ng bahay noong Sabado. — past / nakalipas
3. Kumain kami ng tanghalian — past / nakalipas
4. Kumakanta ako ng aking paboritong awitin. — present / pangkasalukuyan
5. Magbabakasyon kami sa Baguio. — future / hinaharap
6. Siya ay nagtapos ng kolehiyo kahapon. — past / nakalipas
7. Si Ana ay nag-aaral ng kasaysayan. — present / pangkasalukuyan
8. Ang aking kuya ay nagmamaneho ng sasakyan. — present / pangkasalukuyan
9. Bibili ako ng tinapay mamaya. — future / hinaharap
10. Nagturo ng aralin ang guro. — past / nakalipas

Section 5 - Exercise #5

A. **Daily Activities**

1. Ang iyong nanay ay natutulog. / Natutulog ang iyong nanay. / Ang nanay mo ay natutulog. / Natutulog ang nanay mo.
2. Huwag kang kumain ng kanin.
3. Ang batang lalaki ay nagsisipilyo. / Nagsisipilyo ang batang lalaki.
4. Ako ay mag-eehersisyo bukas. / Mag-eehersisyo ako bukas.
5. Humiga ka sa kama.

At School

6. Ang guro ay natuturo ng Ingles ngayon. / Nagtuturo ng Ingles ang guro ngayon.
7. Ang batang babae ay nagsusulat ng kaniyang pangalan. / Nagsusulat ng kaniyang pangalan ang batang babae. / Ang batang babae ay nagsusulat ng pangalan niya. / Nagsusulat ng pangalan niya ang batang babae.

8. Ang mga estudyante ay magbabasa ng libro. / Magbabasa ng libro ang mga estudyante.
9. Ang lahat sa klase ay tumahimik. / Tumahimik ang lahat sa klase.
10. Si Shane ay nagtatanong sa kaniyang kaklase tungkol sa pagsusulit. / Nagtatanong si Shane sa kaniyang kaklase tungkol sa pagsusulit.

At the Office

11. Nagtatrabaho ka ba bilang sekretarya?
12. Si G. Lim ay nag-utos sa akin na gawin ito. / Nag-utos si G. Lim sa akin na gawin ito.
13. Gagawin ko ang aking trabaho. / Gagawin ko ang trabaho ko.

Leisure Activities/Hobbies

14. Ang mga bata ay kumakanta. / Kumakanta ang mga bata.
15. Si Michael ay tutula mamaya. / Tutula si Michael mamaya.

Feelings/State

16. Naiinis ako sa iyo.
17. Malulungkot ako kapag umalis ka.
18. Naaawa ka ba sa aso ng kapitbahay?

Physical Condition/Sensation

19. Ang kaibigan ko ay nauuhaw. / Nauuhaw ang kaibigan ko.
20. Pinapawisan ako dahil naiinitan ako dito.

B.
1. **c.** Mag-dadrive
2. **a.** Nag-beach
3. **b.** Nagla-laptop
4. **c.** Magbe-bake
5. **a.** Nag-text
6. **a.** Nagka-migraine
7. **c.** Magfu-football
8. **c.** Magkaka-promotion
9. **a.** Nag-tequila
10. **a.** Nag-promise

Section 5 - Listening #2

1. grieving
2. wondering
3. loving
4. annoyed
5. confused
6. tempted
7. will give up
8. will wonder
9. will doubt
10. will love

SECTION 6

Section 6 - Exercise #1

1. **a.** matamis
2. **d.** maasim
3. **c.** maanghang
4. **e.** mapait
5. **a.** matamis
6. **b.** maalat
7. **d.** maasim
8. **b.** maalat
9. **e.** mapait
10. **c.** maanghang

Section 6 - Exercise #2

1. baboy
2. hipon
3. baka
4. prutas
5. sabaw
6. isda
7. kanin
8. manok
9. gulay
10. panghimagas

Section 6 - Listening #1

1. Masarap ang **sinampalukan**.
2. **Ginisa** na niya ang sibuyas.
3. Malinamnam ang itlog na **nilaga**.
4. Humiling siya ng **inihaw** na baboy.
5. Paborito kong ulam ang **tinolang** manok.

1. Malaki ang nabingwit kong **isda**.
2. Tumapon ang **sabaw**.
3. Ang **prutas** ay hinog na.
4. **Baka** ba ang nabinili mo?
5. Hindi ako kumakain ng **hipon**.

SECTION 7

Section 7 - Exercise #1

1. **c.** bumbero
2. **a.** karpintero
3. **b.** tsuper
4. **b.** mananahi
5. **c.** abogado
6. **a.** guro
7. **c.** tubero
8. **b.** beterinaryo
9. **a.** parmasista
10. **b.** arkitekto

Section 7 - Exercise #2

1. doktor
2. politiko
3. inhinyero
4. mag-aaral
5. sundalo
6. nars
7. magsasaka
8. pulis
9. kartero
10. pintor

Section 7 - Listening #1

1. Kumakain ng avocado ang **abogado**.
2. Sinundo ng **sundalo** ang pangulo.
3. Dumating ng nakasakay sa motor ang **doktor**.
4. Hinahabol ng **pulis** ang magnanakaw.
5. Nakasuot ng sombrero ang **bumbero**.
6. Nakita kong galing sa bahay ninyo ang **kartero**.
7. Ang **magsasaka** ay mabilis na umahon sa bukid.
8. Ipinagmamalaki ko na ako'y isang **manggagawa**.
9. Ang mga **politiko** ay nakamayan ko.
10. Magaling na **arkitekto** ang tatay ko.

SECTION 8

Section 8 - Exercise #1

1. Tila
2. akala
3. palagay
4. akala
5. Tila
6. palagay
7. akala
8. tila
9. akala
10. palagay

Section 8 - Listening #1

1. Sa **palagay** ko, mahal na kita.
2. **Akala** mo hindi ko pansin?
3. **Tila** hihina din ang ulan.
4. Sa **akala** mo, malilinlang mo ako?
5. Ang kaniyang tinuring ay **tila** makatotohanan.
6. Ang aking **palagay** ay nagkamali.
7. **Tila** mahihirapan bumangon ang mundo sa pandemya.
8. Sa aking **palagay**, ikaw ay masaya.
9. Ang **akala** ko'y hinahanap ka niya.
10. Ang kaniyang iniisip ay **tila** kakaiba.

MORE BOOKS BY LINGO MASTERY

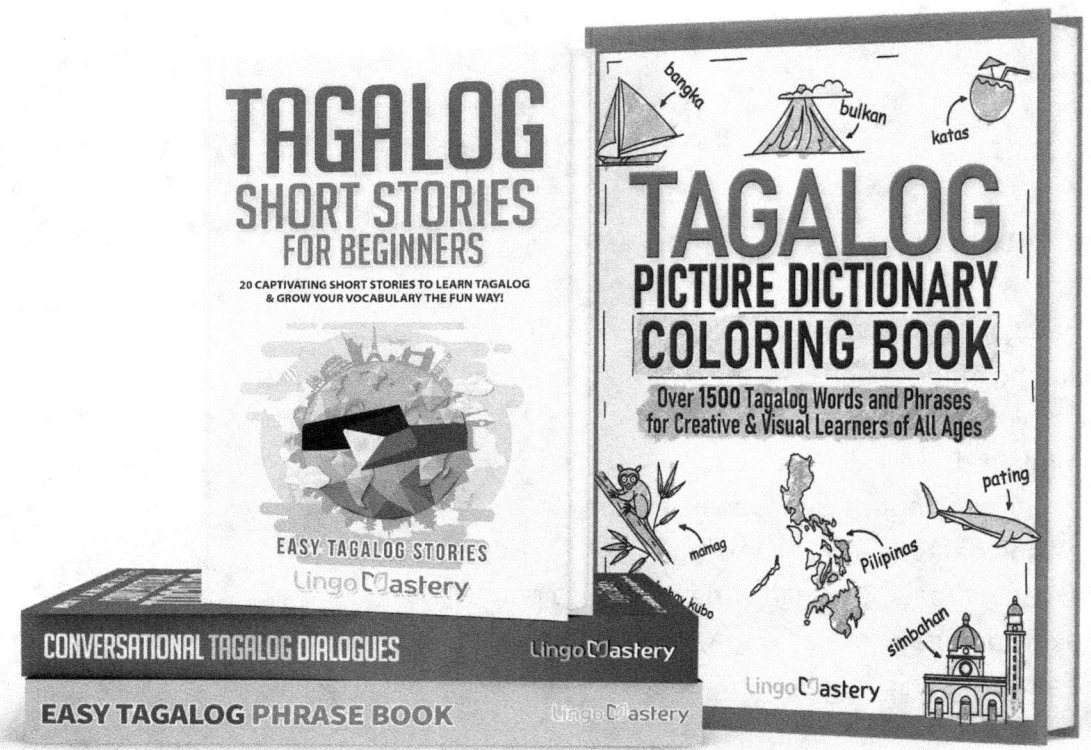

We are not done teaching you Tagalog until you're fluent!

Here are some other titles you might find useful in your journey of mastering Tagalog:

✓ Tagalog Short Stories for Beginners

✓ Intermediate Tagalog Short Stories

✓ 2000 Most Common Tagalog Words in Context

✓ Conversational Tagalog Dialogues

But we got many more!

Check out all of our titles at **www.LingoMastery.com/Tagalog**

www.ingramcontent.com/pod-product-compliance
Lightning Source LLC
Chambersburg PA
CBHW081446070526
44586CB00019B/2251